Beautiful WORD™ BIBLE STUDIES

SONG OF SONGS

THE LOVE WE LONG FOR

BIBLE STUDY GUIDE + STREAMING VIDEO

SEVEN SESSIONS

LISA HARPER

HarperChristian Resources

Song of Songs Beautiful Word Bible Study

Published by HarperChristian Resources, 3950 Sparks Drive SE, Suite 101, Grand Rapids, MI 49546, USA. HarperChristian Resources is a registered trademark of HarperCollins Christian Publishing, Inc.

Requests for information should be addressed to customercare@harpercollins.com.

ISBN 978-0-310-16945-1 (softcover)
ISBN 978-0-310-16946-8 (ebook)

HarperChristian Resources titles may be purchased in bulk for church, business, fundraising, or ministry use. For information, please email ResourceSpecialist@ChurchSource.com.

Lisa Harper is represented by Alive Literary Agency, www.aliveliterary.com.

HarperCollins Publishers, Macken House, 39/40 Mayor Street Upper, Dublin 1, D01 C9W8, Ireland (https://www.harpercollins.com).

Art Direction: Ron Huizinga
Cover Design: Michelle Lenger
Interior Design: Thinkpen Design

First Printing March 2026 / Printed in the United States of America

CONTENTS

WELCOME

Beautiful WORD™ BIBLE STUDIES

SONG OF SONGS

THE LOVE WE LONG FOR

SOMETIMES the Bible can seem overwhelming. Where do you go for words of comfort when you're feeling overwhelmed, lost, or frustrated in life? What book of the Bible do you turn to for wisdom about the situation you find yourself in?

The *Beautiful Word Bible Studies* series makes the Bible come alive in such a way that you know where to turn no matter where you find yourself in your spiritual journey.

Song of Songs, sometimes called Song of Solomon, is a poem that captures a beautiful love story between two characters: Solomon and Shulamite. The descriptions in this book are pretty scandalous, as readers walk with them through their courtship, wedding day, and marriage. Song of Songs is usually reserved for marriage conferences or books about relationships. But not this time! Between the racy descriptions of their love and the drama of a new relationship, we find an underlying message of unconditional love.

Song of Songs is likely rooted in history and relevant for us today. It describes a very real, very intimate relationship between King Solomon and his beloved, Shulamite (although some scholars choose to teach the Songs solely as allegory). Solomon was the third king of Israel, son of King David, who led God's people into a time of wealth, power, and unprecedented peace. We know Solomon was infatuated with love . . . by the end of his life he had hundreds of wives. But at this moment in history, he only has eyes for one: Shulamite.

While Solomon's and Shulamite's love for one another captures the history of this poem, it doesn't give us a full picture of the *meaning*. Rabbi Akiva, a second-century rabbinic leader, called Song of Songs the "holy of holies" of Scripture.[1] In other words, this book of the Bible is *so sacred* that it deserves to be set apart as such. Why? It points us deeper than erotic poetry. It points us to the unending, unconditional love of God. It shows us that we, God's people, are His beloved.

For Christians, when we interpret Song of Songs through the lens of Christ (also called a Christological interpretation), we find an allegory of Christ calling us His beloved. We find a beautiful poem that reflects to us the love Christ, as the Divine Bridegroom, has for us, His bride. The rich descriptions of adoration and devotion come alive and rightly situate Scripture as a divine love story, with Song of Songs expressing that love wholly.

Our invitation is to read Song of Songs both in its historical context (after all, it *is* an erotic love story) *and* through a Christological lens. And as we do, to allow Holy Spirit to probe our hearts and ask the question: Do I truly believe I am the beloved of Christ?

In Song of Songs, the rich descriptions of adoration and devotion come alive and rightly situate Scripture as a divine love story.

HOW TO USE THIS GUIDE

GROUP INFORMATION

The *Beautiful Word Song of Songs* video study is designed to be experienced as a group, in settings like Bible studies, small groups, or Sunday school classes. Each group session starts off with an opening activity designed to break the ice and kick-start group engagement. Then, the group will watch a video together featuring Lisa Harper and move into a time of small group discussion. Outlines are provided for participants if group members want to take notes during the video. Leaders can decide, based on the needs of the group or the direction of the conversation, how many questions to discuss during the group discussion time. Not all questions need to be discussed or answered.

MATERIALS

Instructions for video viewing can be found on the inside of the front cover of this study guide. The video is available via streaming or a DVD is available for purchase. Each participant should have a copy of this study guide to follow along during group sessions and to complete the personal study days in between group sessions.

LEADER GUIDANCE AND TIMING

This study guide includes notes for the leader of the group that instruct them on which sections to read aloud and how long they should aim for each section to last. The video outline notes and group discussion questions are designed so that anyone can lead a group and follow along with each group study element. Between group meetings, participants can complete the personal study days and Scripture memorization. There is also a Beautiful Word coloring page to go with each week's material.

Timing is flexible and the timing notes are there as a general guide. If the group does not have sufficient time for the entirety of the group session, it can be helpful to ask group members to view the week's video ahead of time to save time during the group session. Use the leader's guide in the back of this study for additional guidance on timing and group facilitation. *Leaders should look ahead at the next week's opening activity, as there may be materials or setup required.*

PERSONAL STUDY

Because each group member should have his or her own study guide, they can work through the personal study days in between the group sessions. These personal study days are designed to supplement the conversation that occurred during the previous group session and invite participants into additional Scripture study and personal reflection. Participants who complete each personal study day of this guide will read through the entirety of Song of Songs!

The personal study days are not designed to be shared in the group sessions, so participants can feel freedom to reflect on the content in ways that work best for them. Personal study each week should take about two hours cumulatively, so participants can plan accordingly. If a participant cannot complete the personal study days (or only completes part of them), they should still plan to attend the next group session! Personal study is meant to supplement the experience but should not be treated as mandatory homework.

THRIVING GROUPS

Group study can be incredibly rewarding as group members are invited to learn together and grow in their faith, in community. To create a group space that facilitates this kind of growth, be mindful of the kind of environment you want to create. Group members should be encouraged to commit to attending each session to create consistency and build trust.

Additionally, be intentional about creating safety in conversation by listening well, validating the responses of others, and encouraging each member to contribute to discussion. Work to help each person feel heard and seen and try to resist the temptation to "fix" someone's thoughts or ideas (even if they seem a little confusing or theologically off). Consider articulating a group agreement or covenant at the start of the study so that all members are on the same page and are committed to creating a space that will lead to friendship, growth, and community.

Note: If you are leading the group, there are additional resources in the back of this study guide to help you lead a discussion group.

SESSION 1

INTO ME YOU SEE

GROUP SESSION

SONG OF SONGS

Opening Group Activity (10-15 MINUTES)

WHAT YOU'LL NEED:

☑ A notecard for each person
☑ Pens or markers

1. Each participant is invited to write down the name or description of one of their favorite love stories. It could be from a book, a movie, a song, a cultural story, or their own life. On the other side of the notecard, each participant should write down words or phrases that come to mind when they reflect on that story.

   Example: (front of card) Romeo and Juliet, (back of card) desire, longing, passion

2. After each participant decides on their love story and writes down their descriptive words, discuss the following questions:

   Why is that story one of your favorites?

   What words/phrases did you write on your card and why?

   What common themes or patterns did you notice from each participants' choices?

   Do any of those themes reflect the love of God for you? Why or why not?

SCRIPTURE COVERED IN THIS SESSION:

JEREMIAH 2:1-2; ISAIAH 54:5-7; EPHESIANS 5:25, 32; REVELATION 19:6-8; LUKE 24:13-21, 27; SONG OF SONGS 1:2-4

Watch Session One Video (37 MINUTES)

Leader, play the video using the streaming access code found on the inside front cover of the study guide or use the DVD. As you watch, take notes on anything that stands out to you.

God loves you very intimately, even when you shrink back from His embrace.

Some scholars prefer to consider Song of Songs as psalms and wisdom literature together.

The title, Song of Songs, is a Hebrew superlative (best song ever!). Rabbi Akiva describes this book as the Bible's "holy of holies."[2]

Scholars who considered Song of Songs one of the most important books in the canon: Origen (AD 185–254), St. Jerome (c. AD 347–420), Martin Luther (1483–1546), Dietrich Bonhofeffer (1906–1945)

Five biblical interpretations (senses/styles/methods): allegory, drama, political, literal, or mythical/cultic

Marital language is used throughout Scripture for God's relationship with us.

A Christological interpretation considers the historical significance of the text (literal) then moves into how the text informs our relationship with Christ using symbolism (allegorical).

The man and woman of Song of Songs are King Solomon and a woman named Shulamite (the male version of Solomon's name).

It is surprising that Shulamite starts the story, which would have been considered culturally shameful in the tenth century BCE.

θεόπνευστος (*theopneustos*) means "God-breathed." All Scripture is God-breathed, including Song of Songs.

Song of Songs is a declaration of the level of intimacy Christ wants with us (Jeanne Guyon, in the 1700s, was imprisoned for saying so).[3]

Group Discussion Questions (30-45 MINUTES)

Leader Note: Spend time discussing the questions below together. As the leader, you can decide which questions to discuss, allowing flexibility for conversation and group interest.

1. For many of us, Song of Songs is a book we only hear about in the context of marriage. What experience, if any, have you had with Song of Songs?

   When you think of this book, what comes to mind for you?

   How do you feel about framing Song of Songs as informing our view of our relationship with God?

2. Select a volunteer to **read Song of Songs 1:1–3** aloud to the group.

   What word or phrase that Shulamite uses to describe her beloved stands out to you? Why?

3. Lisa talked about how she has sometimes viewed God as disappointed in her, causing her to strive to "do better, be better." Have you ever been tempted to frame your relationship with God as one of constant striving?

   Why do you think that seeing God that way hinders our relationship with Him?

Jesus came to delight in us. That delight is reflected in the poetic descriptions in Song of Songs.

4. Have a participant **read Luke 24:25–27** out loud to the group. The interpretive method, or style, we will be using for studying Song of Songs is what is called the Christological (or Jesus-centered) lens. Christological interpretation combines literal and allegorical interpretations.

   How familiar are you with the idea of interpreting Scripture through a Jesus-centered lens?

   Can you think of other stories in the Old Testament that point to Jesus or tell us about Him in an indirect way like Song of Songs?

5. Many Scriptures utilize marital language to describe God's relationship with His people. Select a volunteer to **read Ephesians 5:25–32**.

   What are two to three aspects of marriage that help us better understand God's relationship with us?

6. The metaphor of Christ as the Bridegroom and the body of believers as Christ's bride is a beautiful picture throughout Scripture that uses relational intimacy to express Christ's love for us. Select volunteers to look up and **read Genesis 2:24**, **Ephesians 5:25–29**, **2 Corinthians 11:2**, **Revelation 19:7–9**, **Acts 20:28**, and **Isaiah 54:5** aloud to the group.

   What is one practical step you can take this week to lean deeper into the embrace of Christ, as Christ's bride?

Closing Prayer

Consider these prompts as you pray together for:

- An openness to receive God's love in new and more intimate ways
- God's Spirit to challenge each of you to reflect on the areas in your life where God's love is harder to believe
- A commitment to lean deeper into God's embrace throughout this study

Preparation

To prepare for the next group session:

1. **Read Song of Songs chapter 1** in its entirety one time before beginning your homework.
2. Tackle the next three days of the Session 1 Personal Study.
3. Memorize this week's passage using the Beautiful Word Scripture memory coloring page. As a bonus, look up the Scripture memory passage in different translations and take note of the variations.
4. If you've agreed to bring something for the next session's Opening Group Activity, get it ready.

What comes into our *minds* when we think about *God* is the most *important* thing about us.[4]

—A. W. Tozer

Let him *kiss* me with the kisses of his mouth—for your *love* is more delightful than *wine*.

—Song of Songs 1:2

SESSION 1

personal STUDY TIME

DIGGING INTO THE Beautiful WORD™ BIBLE STUDIES

SONG OF SONGS

INTO ME YOU SEE

Day 1

INTRODUCTION (PART 1)

Song of Songs is a beautiful poem written about the love between two characters: Solomon and Shulamite. These historical figures—Solomon being the third king of Israel during the United Kingdom era (c. 1050–931 BCE)—employ rich, and often sexually charged, language to describe their love for one another. The immediate context of this poetry can leave the reader befuddled, uncomfortable, and even avoidant of the text. For many of us, we have only encountered Song of Songs at a marriage conference or maybe during a sermon series about relationships. Rarely are we invited to study the text ourselves, for its own sake.

But Song of Songs is not just an ancient erotic poem. Throughout Jewish and Christian history, teachers and theologians have noted the significance of a love poem as holy Scripture. The whole of the Bible utilizes marital language as a metaphor for God's love for His people. So, the question is begged, if God put a love poem smack in the middle of the story He inspired to share with us His character, His heart, His faithfulness, purpose, and plan, what does He want us to know about His love for us in this one single book?

1. Have you heard any preaching or teaching on Song of Songs prior to this study? If so, list the context of that teaching below and reflect on where this book tends to "show up" in our faith today.

All Scripture is God-breathed and is useful for teaching, rebuking, correcting and training in righteousness.

2 Timothy 3:16–17

2. When you think of the Song of Songs, what emotions come up for you? Excitement? Embarrassment? Concern? Uncertainty? List your top emotions below and then write a prayer releasing them to God.

3. **Read 2 Timothy 3:16–17**. If all Scripture is God-breathed, as 2 Timothy states, what does that tell us about Song of Songs?

4. The following chart lists several renowned theologians who believe Song of Songs to be an essential text.

Theologian	Time Period
Origen	AD 185–254
Jerome	AD 347–420
Luther	AD 1483–1546
Bonhoeffer	AD 1906–1945

Read Hebrews 12:1 and imagine a *"great cloud of witnesses"* giving you permission to study and even enjoy Song of Songs. Journal your response to that image below.

5. Fill in the following chart as you reflect on God using marriage as a metaphor of His love for His people.

Marriage Means:	God Shows This Attribute to Me By:
Commitment	
Love	
Intimacy	
Security	
Sacrifice	

6. The sexuality expressed in Song of Songs can cause some discomfort or embarrassment, yet many theologians cite this book as central to our understanding of God's love for us. Mark your level of comfort with Song of Songs along the spectrum below.

❶ ← ❷ — ❸ — ❹ — ❺ — ❻ — ❼ — ❽ — ❾ → ❿

I'm really uncertain/nervous. I'm open but hesitant. I'm all in.

7. Write a prayer, asking God to journey with you in this study and to reveal His love to you through this book.

Day 2

INTRODUCTION (PART 2)

In order to study Song of Songs well, it is helpful to understand the context of the time period during which the book is set. It is also important to think about the genre of the book and how that contributes to our interpretation of it. Solomon was the king of Israel at the height of Israel's wealth and political power in that time. He had a lavish palace, built the temple of God, and eventually had so many wives that God sent judgment on him. But before his downfall, he appears in this poetry with a woman he loves, Shulamite.

The fact that this book is poetry means it is interpreted in a distinct way. Poems employ heightened language: simile, metaphor, or hyperbole, for example. Poems utilize structure and repetition to communicate deeper truths. So, it is important to keep this in mind as we read through Song of Songs. Much like we would not turn to assigned English literature for help studying for our math test, we should not ask a poem to do something it is not written to do!

1. Read the chart below and **circle** the methods that are described in the introductory video this week.

Method	How You Read Song of Songs
Allegory	The book is *only* a metaphor for Christ and the church.
Drama	The book is like a play.
Political	The book is a celebration of Solomon's rule as king.
Literal/Historical	The book is *only* a historical love story.
Mythical/Cultic	The book is the biblical response to ancient erotic poetry.

2. In light of these interpretive lenses, the Christological lens will be used in this study. This means we can utilize both allegory and history to interpret the text. List an example of a story from the Bible that can be interpreted both as historical and also as reflective of Christ.

"For your Maker is your husband— the LORD Almighty is his name—the Holy One of Israel is your Redeemer; he is called the God of all the earth."

Isaiah 54:5

3. What does it look like for you to interpret Song of Songs in light of the love of Christ?

   How comfortable are you with this interpretive method?

4. Context is important when studying Scripture because it helps us interpret passages well! What is one part of Solomon's historical context you are excited to learn more about?

5. How do you think Song of Songs being a book of poetry will influence the ways you read each chapter?

6. King Solomon lived during the height of the United Kingdom of Israel (c. 1050—931 BCE). This was the most peaceful, abundant, and flourishing time in Israelite history as promised to David by God. There had never been a kingdom of greater power or wealth or unity than the United Kingdom of Israel under King Solomon.[5] In what ways do you think the difference in the status of Solomon and Shulamite impacts your understanding of this love story as representative of the relationship you have with God?

7. Fill in the blanks below, then journal about the attributes you filled in.

   A love poem in the Bible teaches me that God is ______________________.

   A love poem in the Bible teaches me that God is ______________________.

   A love poem in the Bible teaches me that God is ______________________.

Day 3

READ SONG OF SONGS 1:1–4

The first four verses of Song of Songs (after the introduction of the book in verse 1) are poetic verse from the perspective of the woman. This woman, Shulamite, is Solomon's true love, and she describes her deep passion and love for him. Solomon in this poetry is *the* King Solomon, king over all of Israel. He falls in love with Shulamite, a woman with no royal status and who is much more lowly compared to him. He could have had any woman, but he chose and desires her. She may have been a servant at some point in his father's palace, or he may have simply seen her from afar and loved her. Don't ever forget, Solomon's status in contrast to Shulamite's mirrors the God of the universe being in love with you!

Notice the heightened language that is common in poetry and the way Shulamite describes the depth of their love in these very first verses. ***"Your love is better than wine"*** (ESV), she declares. While they are not yet married, it is clear from the start that Shulamite has felt love from Solomon and is experiencing a deep longing to be with him, not sexually, much more intimately and personally than the flesh. One thing Origen noted over and again in his commentary on Song of Songs was how the relationship described was so much greater than a bodily experience; it was deeply spiritual.[6]

Just as Adam and Eve were separated from the original nearness and union with God in the garden, we, too, feel a separation from Him ongoing in our souls. We long to be with Him, and Shulamite is expressing that sense in these opening verses. It's interesting to note also that the allegorical interpretation of these opening verses is that Shulamite represents the soul's quest for God and a deep relationship with the divine.

1. **Read verses 2–3** slowly. Think about the purpose of poetry. While poetry can be analyzed, it is also meant to be treasured and experienced. Treasure and experience verses 2–3, first from the perspective of the woman and then from your perspective as you meditate on your relationship with God.

   How does slow meditation on these verses enhance its meaning for you?

2. In the ancient world, perfumes were expensive and beautifully fragrant. What do you think it means that Shulamite compares Solomon's name to perfume?

What would a modern-day comparison be that expresses that kind of love?

All Scripture points us to *Christ.*

3. It is very countercultural that the woman's voice would begin this poem. She is the one seen longing for and even pursuing the man in these early verses. Why do you think the author chose to highlight her voice at the start of this book?

4. **Read verse 4** below and circle each verb.

(She)
Take me away with you—let us hurry!
Let the king bring me into his chambers.

(Friends)
We rejoice and delight in you;
we will praise your love more than wine.

(She)
How right they are to adore you!

What kind of love do you think this is based on the verbs you circled? Is their love calm? Detached? Frenzied? Passionate? Describe what it sounds like to you.

Take me away with you—let us hurry! Let the king bring me into his chambers.

Song of Songs 1:4

5. **Isaiah 54:5** says,

"For your Maker is your husband—
the Lord Almighty is his name—
the Holy One of Israel is your Redeemer;
he is called the God of all the earth."

In the book of Genesis, God chooses Abraham to be the father of His chosen people, Israel. God makes a promise to Abraham, and later to Moses in Exodus, that He will be Israel's God and they will be His people. These promises are called covenants. They are sacred promises, much like a marriage vow.

At the time of Isaiah, God's people are fully in a covenant with Him, and Isaiah is challenging God's people to live out that covenant faithfully.

Knowing Isaiah used marriage as a metaphor for God's relationship with His people, what does that tell us about God? List the top three attributes of God that this metaphor evokes for you. Then describe why.

-
-
-

Why?

6. With Isaiah 54:5 in mind, return to **Song of Songs 1:1–4**. Reread the passage and notice each time the language evokes love, passion, and belonging in a relationship.

   How does Song of Songs invite us to meditate on God's love for His people? And for us?

7. Today's scripture, verses 1–4, invites us to imagine the longing of the woman as our own longing for intimacy with Christ. Write a prayer in the following space that reflects your own longing for God as the bride of Christ.

Reflection

As you reflect on the history, significance, context, and impact of Song of Songs, what are the **BEAUTIFUL WORDS** the Holy Spirit has been highlighting to you through this time? Write or draw them in the space below.

SESSION
2

STOPPED IN YOUR TRACKS

GROUP SESSION

SONG OF SONGS

Opening Group Activity (10–15 MINUTES)

WHAT YOU'LL NEED:

- ☑ Four sticky notes per person
- ☑ A poster or whiteboard with two columns, one that says "our eyes" and the other that says "God's eyes"
- ☑ Pens or dry-erase markers

1. Each participant is invited to write down two insecurities they walk with when it comes to their faith, relationships, or personhood. Phrases like "I'm too much" or "I'm unqualified" or "I'm not good enough" might come to mind. Feel welcome to be as creative and as vulnerable as you would like.
2. Each participant is then invited to write down two truths about them that they know from God. Phrases like "God delights in me" or "I am enough" might come to mind. Like before, feel welcome to write whatever comes to you.
3. Each participant will then put their two insecurities up on the poster under the "our eyes" column and their two truths up under the "God's eyes" column.
4. After each participant places their sticky notes on the poster, discuss the following questions:

   What stands out to you or what do you notice about the "our eyes" column? How would you compare that to the "God's eyes" column?

   Why do you think it's easier to believe the "our eyes" column as opposed to the "God's eyes" column?

   What is one truth you see in the "God's eyes" column that you can bring to God in prayer and ask Him to cement within your heart as truth this week?

SCRIPTURE COVERED IN THIS SESSION: SONG OF SONGS 1:5–6, 8–10, 15; 2:3–5

Watch Session Two Video (27 MINUTES)

Leader, stream the video or play the DVD. As you watch, take notes on anything that stands out to you.

- Throughout church history, this book wasn't just a side dish; it was a main entrée of theology for leaders like Origen and Bonhoeffer.

- The Christological approach is our lens—seeing the text through the redemptive work of Jesus.

- In chapter 1, Shulamite takes a turn toward insecurity, questioning why the king would ever love someone like her.

- She describes herself as "dark" from working in the fields, contrasting her lowly status with Solomon's royalty.

- Just like Shulamite, we often let others speak into our lives in ways that contradict God's love for us.

God looks at us through rose-colored glasses that have been tinted red through the blood of Jesus Christ.

—Lisa Harper

- Solomon's voice declares she is the most beautiful; he adores her and will not even entertain her insecurities (Song of Songs 1:8–11, 15).

- Shulamite reflects on their love for one another (2:3–13) and mentions the "banqueting house," signaling that Solomon is taking their relationship public.

- Solomon's love for Shulamite is like God's love for us: unencumbered and unashamed.

- We are seated in a place of honor with God. He claims us, loves us, delights in us.

- We are invited to contemplate the areas of our lives that are hard for us to believe God could love . . . and bring them straight to God.

Group Discussion Questions (30–45 MINUTES)

Leader Note: Spend time discussing the questions below together. As the leader, you can decide which questions to discuss, allowing flexibility for conversation and group interest.

1. **Read Song of Songs 1:5–7.** What stands out to you about Shulamite's statements?

2. Shulamite's status is much lower than King Solomon's, and it seems like she feels insecure, a bit unlovable, or perhaps undeserving of such esteemed love. How does Shulamite's status compare to ours before God? Have you ever felt like Shulamite?

3. **Read Song of Songs 1:9–11.** Solomon is delighted in Shulamite and does not even acknowledge her protests or insecurities. What does that tell us about their relationship? What does that tell you about how God sees His relationship with you?

4. Reading this poetry through a Christological lens, Solomon's declarations can be compared to Christ as our Bridegroom. Describe a time when you felt wholly loved by God. How can you carry that feeling into your daily life?

5. Ask God to reveal any places in your relationship with Him where it's hard for you to really believe that a Bridegroom like Him would want a bride like you. What are some of those areas of your life?

6. **Read Song of Songs 2:4.** Solomon makes his relationship with Shulamite "public" in this verse. In what ways might God demonstrate His love for each of us publicly?

Closing Prayer

Consider these prompts as you pray together for:

- God to reveal the places in our lives where we struggle to accept His love
- Grace to love one another by embodying the depth of love God has for us
- Peace within our hearts and souls as we dwell on God's delight in us

Preparation

To prepare for the next group session:

1. **Read Song of Songs chapters 1–2** in their entirety one time before doing your homework.
2. Tackle the next three days of the Session 2 Personal Study.
3. Memorize this week's passage using the Beautiful Word Scripture memory coloring page. As a bonus, look up the Scripture memory passage in different translations and take note of the variations.
4. If you've agreed to bring something for the next session's Opening Group Activity, get it ready.

Let him lead me
to the banquet hall, and let
his banner over me be

SESSION

2

personal STUDY TIME

DIGGING INTO THE

Beautiful WORD™ BIBLE STUDIES

SONG OF SONGS

INTO ME YOU SEE

Day 1

READ SONG OF SONGS 1:5–11

The voice of the man, Solomon, appears in today's Scripture passage. Solomon compares Shulamite's beauty to that of a mare and then says she deserves gold and silver jewelry. Historically, the comparison of his lover to a mare among Pharaoh's chariots is interesting, as the chariots would have most likely been pulled by stallions (not mares). So, in this section of the poem, Solomon is saying she is as desirous as one mare amongst hundreds of stallions. As we study these verses today, we will explore what they reveal about desire, identity, and the way love makes us feel chosen, unique, and treasured.

1. **Read verses 5–6.** Here, Shulamite describes her skin color as darkened by the sun. A description like this may be in reference to her being out in the sun as a necessity. In fact, she describes being forced to tend to the vineyards, meaning she is of a lower status than Solomon. She even says, ***"Do not gaze at me"*** (ESV), because she has spent so much time tending the vineyards and is ashamed of her status.

   List two to three experiences in your life that you would prefer to hide from God (like Shulamite wanting to hide her tending of the vineyards). After each one, write a one-sentence prayer, asking God for faith to believe He wants to see us fully.

   -
   -
   -

2. **Read verse 7.** Shulamite ends her opening to this poem by seeking to know where her lover's flocks are, so that she can be with him. Seeking the flocks of her lover paints him as a shepherd. The image of a shepherd in the Bible is one of care and attentiveness. King Solomon's father, David, was a shepherd prior to becoming king. It is possible this statement is metaphorical, positioning Solomon, as king of Israel, as the shepherd to God's people. It also may be literal, as a king would have had many flocks and fields.

Shulamite goes on to ask, *"Why should I be as one who veils herself by the flocks?"* (NKJV). Culturally, she is saying, "I do not want to just be one of many. I do not want to be just 'among the flocks.'" She seeks Solomon as he shepherds and wants him exclusively.

If you have had the privilege of knowing an exclusive earthly love, how does learning about the love relationship God wants to have with you change or inform your earthly experience?

If you have not experienced an exclusive earthly love, how does learning God wants you to know exclusive love from and with Him change or affect the way you define the love you desire?

3. **Read verses 8–9.** If you remember from yesterday, Shulamite asks her love where he grazes his flock, implying she wants to seek him there. Verse 8 reads as a response to that request: *"Follow the tracks of the sheep."* Notice how quickly he replies to her, showing his prompt, attentive care for her. If Solomon were a modern-day man, what would be a modern equivalent to "follow the tracks of the sheep"?

   What is a track of the sheep you can follow that will lead you closer to Jesus?

Understanding the socio-historical context of the Song will enhance our understanding and application of this ancient poetry.

—Lisa Harper

4. Solomon declares Shulamite to be so one-of-a-kind that she is a mare among stallions. Imagine Jesus, walking into the room you are in right now, and declaring that over you. That you are so uniquely beloved by Him. That you are God's favorite. Journal your response to Him below.

5. **Read verses 10–11.** Here, Solomon is adorning her with his love. Fill out the following chart.

For	What It Means to Be Adorned by God's Love
Myself	
My friends	
My church	
My enemies	

6. Circle the statements that you love the most about Solomon's response to Shulamite.

His promptness **His adoration** **His adornment of her**

His gifts **His invitation** **His responsiveness**

His declaration of her uniqueness **His love**

Reflect on a significant time when you felt love from someone. What was it like? Have you ever felt that kind of love from God? If so, reflect on that. If not, ask God to reveal that kind of love to you.

7. Inside the circle below, write down some words or phrases that describe how God sees you. If you don't feel sure of how God sees you, write words of how you long to be seen (even if you don't feel like you deserve it). Then, pray through each word you wrote down and ask God for the blessing to come to know His delight in you. (Examples: beautiful, loved, secure)

Beloved

I liken you, my darling, to a mare among Pharaoh's chariot horses.

Song of Songs 1:9

Day 2

READ SONG OF SONGS 1:12–17

Where can I go from your *Spirit?* Where can I flee from your *presence?*

Psalm 139:7

Chapter 1 of Song of Songs finishes with alternating verses between the man and the woman, continuing in their admiration of one another. The poetry engages all the senses, focusing on the scent of the woman's perfume and the imagery of the vineyards of En Gedi.

Here is where learning some context in Bible study becomes so rich. En Gedi, in the ancient world, was a famous oasis, known for its lush greenery. And King Solomon's territory was exponential to that of his father, King David. We are not just talking about minor imagery here; these references are like gazing upon the Hope Diamond from a yacht in the middle of the Pacific Ocean. Vast, magnificently beautiful, worthy of words one can't quite find.

Quite the way to describe one's beloved! Their responses to one another invite the reader to meditate on the richness of their love and, in turn, the richness of God's love for them.

1. **Read Song of Songs 1:12–14.** Notice the focus on the scent of her perfume and imagine how close and intimate one would need to be to notice that scent. Think about a scent that immediately transports you somewhere. How does that scent make you feel?

   How does this image help you picture the closeness of someone you love or who has had great impact on your life?

2. Now **read Psalm 139.** Verse 7 talks about how God's Spirit is always with us. Imagine, in light of Song of Songs, the scent of God's Spirit. As you breathe in and out, is that scent comforting to you? Use all five senses to imagine the closeness of God's Spirit to you and describe each one below. (Examples: I imagine God's Spirit to smell like fresh morning dew. I imagine God's Spirit to feel like a warm hug.)

   Smell: __________

   Touch: __________

   Taste: __________

   Hear: __________

   See: __________

3. **Return to Song of Songs chapter 1 and read verses 15–17.** The lovers describe one another's beauty in these verses. If God were to describe your beauty, what do you long to hear Him say? How might you respond back to God? Write your responses in the chart below.

What I Long to Hear God Say	How I Might Respond

4. **Look up verse 16** in the NIV translation. The woman describes their bed as *verdant*. Verdant (adj.) means green with grass or other lush vegetation.[7] It exudes life and peace. What would your verdant-place with God look like? An oasis? A forest? A beach? A cozy library?

   Psalm 92 gives us an example of how the biblical writers used verdant. **Read Psalm 92:12–15** and then note below who is being described, how, and what this means in connection to how Shulamite uses the same adjective in verse 16.

5. In verse 17, Solomon responds to Shulamite with a description of their house constructed of *"beams . . . of cedar"* and *"rafters of pine."* Some other translations use fir, juniper, or cypress to describe the rafters. Cedar trees grew in Lebanon to the north and were highly valued as building material in the ancient world. Kings used cedar for royal buildings (2 Samuel 5:11; 1 Kings 5:6; 6:9–7:12). It signified royal power and wealth (1 Kings 10:27), growth and strength (Psalm 92:12; Ezekiel 17). Pine, fir, cypress, or juniper all refer to a soft, strong wood with elasticity, fragrance, and usefulness for building.

   How does Solomon's response to Shulamite provide an image for how he reveres their relationship?

   What does his description say about his confidence in their union?

6. Song of Songs uses lots of heightened language (after all, it is poetry!). To prepare for that, return to the earlier verses in Song of Songs 1, and write down examples of imagery you can find in the following chart. (Example: verse 1, wine, Love is even more delightful.)

Verse	Imagery	Interpretation

7. As we close the first chapter, how does chapter 1 invite you to understand and accept how much God delights in you and how intentional He is in describing the love He wants you to know?

Imagine Jesus taking your face in His hands and telling you that you are His favorite. Write a prayer to God sharing wherever your heart is in this moment. He delights in you and wants this relationship desperately.

My *beloved* is to me a cluster of henna *blossoms* from the *vineyards* of En Gedi.

Song of Songs 1:14

Day 3

READ SONG OF SONGS 2:1–4

Chapter 2 of Song of Songs begins with verses that express the delight Solomon and Shulamite have for one another. Up until this point in Song of Songs, the love between Solomon and Shulamite is private, but now, in verses 3–4, we see Solomon declaring his love for Shulamite publicly. Solomon takes her to the banquet house. In ancient times, a banquet house was a place of celebration and feasting. It was very public. A modern-day equivalent would be taking Shulamite out to a very fancy and famous restaurant, for all the paparazzi to see. Remember the T-shirts at the mall . . . "I'm with her" / "I'm with him"?

The passage also says that his banner is over her. It's as if Solomon is unfurling a large sign or flag that reads "We're together now!" Shulamite then continues her adoration of Solomon by describing his embrace as nourishing to her soul.

1. **Read verses 1–3.** In these opening verses, metaphors of flowers and fruit describe each lover's passion for the other. Identify each time a plant or fruit shows up in these three verses by writing each mention below. Then describe the ways this metaphor engaged your senses. The first one is done as an example.

Flower or Fruit	What This Metaphor Makes Me Think Of
Example: rose	Example: beautiful to look at, sweet to smell, romantic, special

2. **Return to chapter 1 and reread verses 5–7. Then read 2:4.** Compare and contrast Solomon and Shulamite's relationship from chapter 1 to chapter 2. (Hint: 2:4 is the verse when Solomon takes their relationship public!)

Song of Songs 1:5–7	Song of Songs 2:4
Example: insecurity	Example: unashamed

3. As their relationship goes public, Shulamite knows that Solomon's banner over her is love. In other words, Solomon declares, loud and proud, that he loves Shulamite. Imagine Christ declaring a banner of love over you. Write down examples of His love for you in the banner image below.

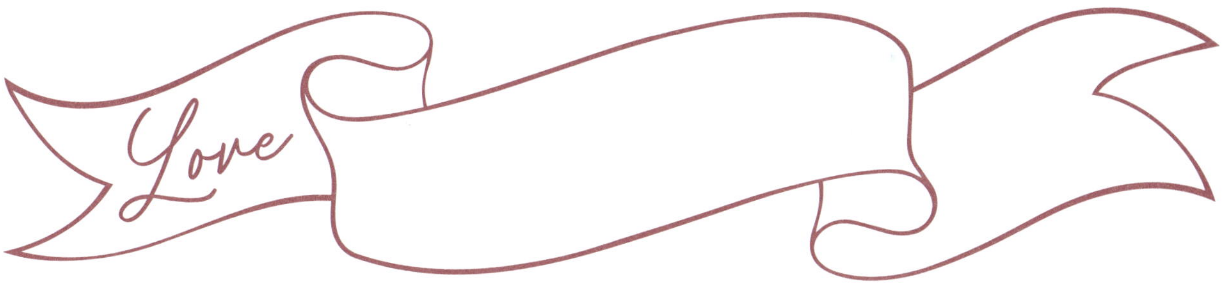

4. Look at the banner you created in question 3 and imagine that banner flying high and proud, as a gesture of God's revealed love for you. Journal below about the emotions you might feel looking up at that banner in a public place.

5. **Romans 8:17** says, *"Now if we are children, then we are heirs—heirs of God and co-heirs with Christ, if indeed we share in his sufferings in order that we may also share in his glory."* In Christ, it is declared that we are in a place of honor, much like Shulamite when she is brought to the banquet hall.
Circle which sentence indicates how secure you feel in the knowledge that you are a co-heir with Christ.

It's hard for me to believe.

I believe it sometimes.

I am fully resting in this truth.

His *banner* over me was *love.*

Song of Songs 2:4 ESV

6. Song of Songs 2:1–4 uses our senses to heighten the descriptions of Solomon and Shulamite's love for one another. Think of three ways you engage your five senses when you worship God and notice how certain sounds, sights, smells, or even tastes invoke feelings of love and warmth. List them below.

•

•

•

7. Write a prayer declaring your own banner of love, publicly, for Christ. What would that banner say and look like?

Reflection

As you reflect on your personal study of Song of Songs 1, what are the **BEAUTIFUL WORDS** the Holy Spirit has been highlighting to you through this time? Write or draw them in the space below.

SESSION
3

SUITORS WHO RUN AND FOXES WHO RUIN

GROUP SESSION

SONG OF SONGS

Opening Group Activity (10–15 MINUTES)

WHAT YOU'LL NEED:

- ☑ One notecard per person
- ☑ Pens or markers

1. Each participant is invited to anonymously write down one act of love they have witnessed or received recently. It could be something small but meaningful like a little text to check in, a home-cooked meal, or someone sitting with them in a moment of pain.
2. The leader will then collect the notecards, shuffle them up, and read a few aloud. After each act of love is read, participants are invited to discuss the following questions:

   What does this gesture tell us about the nature of love?

   How does this gesture paint a picture of someone pursuing or leaning into love?

   What does this gesture reveal to us about our loving God?

SCRIPTURE COVERED IN THIS SESSION:

SONG OF SONGS 2:8–12, 15–17; LUKE 15:11–20; PROVERBS 4:23

Watch Session Three Video (35 MINUTES)

Leader, stream the video or play the DVD. As you watch, take notes on anything that stands out to you.

Song of Songs is one of the Five Scrolls read aloud at the five main Jewish festivals.

Ruth > **Festival of Weeks** > a harvest feast
Ecclesiastes > **Festival of Tabernacles** > a weeklong festival celebrating God's protection
Lamentations > **Tisha B'av** > a fast for the destruction of the temple
Esther > **Purim** > the first spring feast
Song of Songs > **Passover** > a feast commemorating the Jewish escape from Egypt

The second poem moves from the enclosed banqueting house to the vibrant outdoors of spring.

Shulamite's voice leads again, describing her beloved "leaping over the mountains," a poetic picture of his eagerness to be with her.

This isn't a slow, hesitant love; it's an adventurous, passionate pursuit. The imagery is active and full of energy.

Solomon calls for her to "come away with me."

The Bridegroom goes to great lengths to run toward us, much like in the parable of the prodigal son (Luke 15:11–20).

Our God lovingly says, "You're so beautiful today," *and*, "I want you to walk *this* a little bit differently" at the same time.

Jesus dares to depict the man running toward his beloved or the father running toward his son in the parable.

Watchman Nee says in his commentary that, "the passing rain in Song of Songs is a nod to the work of cross being fully accomplished."[8]

What are the little foxes that rob you of your attention in your relationship with Jesus?

Group Discussion Questions (30-45 MINUTES)

Leader Note: Spend time discussing the questions below together. As the leader, you can decide which questions to discuss, allowing flexibility for conversation and group interest.

1. **Read Song of Songs 2:8–10.** These verses serve as a way to picture the lengths God goes to, with great enthusiasm, to move toward us in relationship. What do you notice about this passage that points to God's pursuit of us?

2. Song of Songs is read out loud at Passover. Elie Wiesel said, "I love Passover because for me it is a cry against indifference, a cry for compassion."[9] How do you see Song of Songs 2:8–10 prompting us away from indifference?

3. **Read Luke 15:11–32** (the parable of the prodigal son). Make a list together of everything you would be thinking and feeling as you returned home if you were the prodigal son. How does this list help us to see the father's compassion?

4. Watchman Nee says of Song of Songs 2:8–9, "The Lord is the Lord of resurrection. Christ has resurrected; He has overcome all difficulties and barriers. Difficulties and barriers are things of yesterday. He is living in the next day. All difficulties are beneath His feet. The minute He leaps, all the barriers are behind Him."[10] Where do you see hints of the resurrection in Song of Songs chapter 2? Make a list together of each moment of hope you can find in the chapter.

5. Consider together this question from the video: "What are the foxes that can interrupt our relationship with Jesus?" In other words, what are the seemingly small things that can distract us from God? Discuss them together as a group.

6. **Proverbs 4:23** says, *"Above all else, guard your heart."* What are some ways you can guard your heart against these little foxes?

Closing Prayer

Consider these prompts as you pray together for:

- Our ability to accept a God who runs toward us like Song of Songs 2:8
- God to reveal the little foxes to us
- A desire to guard our hearts from those little foxes and bring our attention and affection back to God

Preparation

To prepare for the next group session:

1. **Read Song of Songs chapters 1–2** in their entirety one time before doing your homework.
2. Tackle the next three days of the Session 3 Personal Study.
3. Memorize this week's passage using the Beautiful Word Scripture memory coloring page. As a bonus, look up the Scripture memory passage in different translations and take note of the variations.
4. If you've agreed to bring something for the next session's Opening Group Activity, get it ready.

Listen! *My beloved!* Look! Here he comes,
leaping across the mountains, bounding over the hills.
—Song of Songs 2:8

SESSION 3

personal STUDY TIME

DIGGING INTO THE

Beautiful WORD™ BIBLE STUDIES

SONG OF SONGS

SUITORS WHO RUN AND FOXES WHO RUIN

Day 1

READ SONG OF SONGS 2:5–7

Verses 5–7 of chapter 2 expand on the love Shulamite feels for Solomon in response to their relationship "going public" in verses 1–4. She describes a love so powerful that it is like a force that, according to verse 7, should not be ***"arous[ed] or awaken[ed] until it so desires."*** The nourishment she finds in Solomon's love and protective stance engage the entire body and all her senses in this moment of admiration.

1. **Read verses 5–6.** What images of God's protection and love come to mind when you read these verses? Write a short prayer below thanking God for nourishing you like Shulamite in the poem.

2. The raisins and apples in verse 5 are sources of strength for Shulamite, considering how lovesick she is. What foods would you choose if you were to describe a desire for nourishment in light of experiencing God's love for you? List them below and then explain why those came to mind.

3. Verse 6 describes Solomon's left arm under Shulamite's head and his right arm embracing her. Picture this and list the qualities of their relationship that this image evokes in the left-hand column below. Then, in the right-hand column, write down one example of how God shows up in your life embodying this quality.

Qualities	How God Shows Up in My Life

4. This section concludes with a warning in **verse 7**:

> ***Daughters of Jerusalem, I charge you by the gazelles and by the does of the field: Do not arouse or awaken love until it so desires.***

In the immediate context, ***"daughters of Jerusalem"*** is likely referring to the young, unmarried women in Shulamite's community. Jerusalem was the capital of Israel, the central city where Solomon would build God's temple and his own palace. So, these women are in that city center and participate in a type of call-and-response in this poetry. In the larger context of Scripture, the ***"daughters of Jerusalem"*** can also refer to God's people as a whole. Complete the following sentences.

Love is powerful for Shulamite because ______________________________.

Love is powerful for Shulamite's community because ______________________________.

Love is powerful for God's people because ______________________________.

Love is powerful for me because ______________________________.

5. In this warning, love is seen as a powerful force that should not be "awakened" prematurely. Where have you seen love show its power in your own life or in your community? Journal about an example below.

6. The progression of verses 1–7 reveals to us a love that is tender, powerful, and even overwhelming. Choose one line from these seven verses that stands out to you and journal below about what it reveals to you about the nature of God's love.

Day 2

READ SONG OF SONGS 2:8–13

Verses 8–13 of chapter 2 give the reader a beautiful picture of Solomon leaping and bounding toward Shulamite through the hills. He will stop at nothing to get to her and is the picture of excitement and exuberance. He calls her forth and tells her to arise, describing the winter rain as passing by, giving way to flowers and springtime. Watchman Nee's commentary of Song of Songs points out to the reader that this imagery reflects the resurrection of Christ. The winter rain (the crucifixion) gives way to the resurrection, filled with flowers, light, and hope. In other words, "there is a shadow of Easter" in this section of Song of Songs 2.[11]

1. **Read Song of Songs 2:8–9.** The picture of Solomon leaping through the hills and mountains, undeterred and fueled by love, is pretty undignified for royalty! Can you imagine a king showing such unrestrained passion? What would you feel if you were Shulamite? Journal below about your own emotional reaction to the king's excitement.

2. Contemplate how you might relate the image in verses 8–9 to your own relationship with God. As you do, fill in the following chart.

In the Poem, Solomon:	In My Life, God:
Leaps across mountains	
Bounds over hills	
Stands at the wall	
Gazes through the windows	
Peers through the lattices	

3. **Song of Songs 2:10** says,

My beloved spoke and said to me,
"Arise, my darling, my beautiful one, come with me."

Picture Jesus standing in your doorway, inviting you to arise and come with Him. How would you respond? Journal your response below.

4. **Read verses 11–12.** In the columns below, create descriptions of the winter rain in verse 11 and the spring renewal in verse 12.

Verse 11: Winter Rain	Verse 12: Spring Renewal
Example: cold	Example: fragrant

5. Images of resurrection appear all throughout the Bible and point us to the resurrection of Christ as the culmination of God's love and redemption of us. Look up and read each of the following passages. Fill in the chart with a brief summary statement of the resurrection imagery the passage conveys.

Read	Summarize Resurrection Imagery
Job 19:25–27	Example: proclamation that God will redeem Job's life
Psalm 49:13–15	
Isaiah 26:19–20	
Ezekiel 37:7–10	

What are some images of resurrection in your own life that point to God's redemptive work? List some below.

6. Verse 13 gives us a refrain, matching the invitation in verse 10. **Read verse 13** and then circle the word or phrase below that most resonates with you when you picture an invitation from God into relationship with Him.

Arise **Come** **My beautiful one** **My darling**

Come with me **Listen!** **Look!** **My beloved**

"See! The winter is past; the rains are over and gone. Flowers appear on the earth; the season of singing has come."

Song of Songs 2:11–12

7. How do you typically respond when God invites you into something new? Do you respond by running toward Him? Running away? Are you excited? Uncertain?

   Reflect on your responses to God's invitations below, and write a short prayer seeking whatever you might need to meet His invitation more openly.

Day 3

READ SONG OF SONGS 2:14–17

Chapter 2 of Song of Songs concludes by returning to the mountains and hills. This time, Solomon speaks and he seeks his beloved in the clefts of the rock. When Shulamite responds to him, she declares that they belong to each other. When he searches for her, he finds her. Verse 15 then warns against the *"little foxes"* that might come and ruin the vineyards. Foxes, in a literal sense, could actually come into a vineyard, dig up the roots of the plants, and utterly destroy the harvest. In this metaphor, the vineyard is their love and these little foxes are the small things that can get in the way of a beautiful relationship. They take their love seriously and want to safeguard it against those things that could creep in and create ruin.

8. **Read verse 14:**

   My dove in the clefts of the rock, in the hiding places on the mountainside, show me your face, let me hear your voice; for your voice is sweet, and your face is lovely.

   Circle each image, metaphor, or description for Shulamite in this verse. What does each picture tell us about Solomon's love for her?

9. **Verse 15** says,

   Catch for us the foxes, the little foxes that ruin the vineyards,
   our vineyards that are in bloom.

   Solomon and Shulamite want to safeguard their relationship so that their love can flourish. What are some of the small things in a romantic relationship that can seem innocuous but ultimately ruin what is most important?

Things that first seem innocuous could actually ruin what is most important to us.

10. What are the little foxes that tend to interrupt your relationship with Jesus? Make a list below and then pray over that list.

-
-
-
-
-

11. **Read verses 16–17.** Shulamite talks about Solomon at daybreak when the shadows flee. Throughout the Bible, God is seen as a bringer of light. In **John 8:12**, Jesus simply says,

"I am the light of the world."

What are the areas of your life where you can invite God to bring light into the shadows?

12. The end of this chapter concludes with an image of Solomon back on the rugged hills mentioned in verse 17. Why do you think the poetry recalls this image twice?

Why do you think this image is so important to Shulamite?

13. Throughout chapter 2, many words are used to describe Solomon and Shulamite's pursuit of one another. Put a check mark next to the words, phrases, or ideas that most resonate with you from this chapter.

- ☐ Feeling pursued
- ☐ Feeling wanted or cherished
- ☐ Feeling hidden or protected
- ☐ Wanting to "arise and come away" (longing for newness)
- ☐ Experiencing spiritual springtime or renewal
- ☐ Feeling seen and heard
- ☐ Needing reassurance

14. Write a prayer asking God to meet you in the midst of your relationship with Him and to bring to light any little foxes that might be getting in the way of your love.

Reflection

As you reflect on your personal study of Song of Songs 2, what are the **BEAUTIFUL WORDS** the Holy Spirit has been highlighting to you through this time? Write or draw them in the space below.

SESSION 4

A BREATHLESS SEARCH AND A BIG PARADE

GROUP SESSION

SONG OF SONGS

Opening Group Activity (10-15 MINUTES)

WHAT YOU'LL NEED:

- ☑ A posterboard or whiteboard
- ☑ Pens or dry-erase markers

1. One participant should draw a T-chart on the board. Label the right-hand column "what gets in the way" and label the left-hand column "what draws us in."

2. Spend some time as a group brainstorming the things that tend to get in the way of our intimacy with Jesus. Then, brainstorm the things that draw us close to Jesus. Participants are encouraged to shout out their suggestions and have someone write them down as they say them.

3. After spending time brainstorming as a group, look at the list and discuss these questions:

   Do you see any common themes in either column? What is showing up in these lists?

   Do you resonate with any particular item on the list?

   When you think about your faith, do you tend to focus on the obstacles to intimacy with God or the invitations to intimacy? Why?

SCRIPTURE COVERED IN THIS SESSION: SONG OF SONGS 3:1-4, 6-11; EXODUS 13:21-22, THE PSALMS OF ASCENT

Watch Session Four Video (30 MINUTES)

Leader, stream the video or play the DVD. As you watch, take notes on anything that stands out to you.

Shulamite is disappointed in chapter 3 and is looking for Solomon but does not find him.

She's preoccupied with the loss of Solomon and goes to great lengths to find him, much like in the story of losing Missy.

After Solomon and Shulamite reunite, the passage immediately pivots to a wedding, in verse 6, which starts with a parade.

Israel is a major political player during this time period, so the wedding would have been lavish, and people would have come from all over the region to celebrate.

Much like Solomon being present with Shulamite from now on, God is present all throughout Israel's history, first in a cloud and pillar.

All throughout the *story* of *Scripture*, God says, "I *love* you. I'm with you. *Come* closer."

—Lisa Harper

Theophany: a physical manifestation of God's presence in Scripture[12]

Shulamite looks upon Solomon, carried by the mighty men, up the hill toward the temple of God.

Solomon's mother, Bathsheba, crowns him with a handmade wreath for his wedding day.

Much like Solomon climbing the hill toward Shulamite, Jesus as our Bridegroom goes to extraordinary lengths for us.

Group Discussion Questions (30–45 MINUTES)

Leader Note: Spend time discussing the questions below together. As the leader, you can decide which questions to discuss, allowing flexibility for conversation and group interest.

1. **Read Song of Songs 3:1–4.** In these verses, Shulamite is frantically searching for Solomon and then finds him and clings to him. What is the closest thing in your life to that longing you have felt? Have you ever felt that way toward God?

2. The relief of their reunion leads immediately to a lavish, wealthy wedding scene. Look through **verses 6–10** as a group and pick out every clue you can find of just how impressive the wedding ceremony was. What do you think this beautiful, ornate wedding says about Solomon's love?

3. **Read Exodus 13:21–22.** As a group, compare and contrast this passage to the picture of Solomon ascending toward Shulamite. How does that ascent give us a picture of God drawing closer to His people? What is one tangible way you can notice God's presence in your own life?

4. Like Solomon going to great lengths to show his love for Shulamite, God will go to great lengths to show His love for us. What is one way God has gone out of His way to show you He loves you?

5. Psalm 121 is an example of a Psalm of Ascent. These psalms were written and sung while traveling to Jerusalem and climbing toward the temple of God. **Read Psalm 121** together and find the parallels to the story of Solomon's wedding.

6. The story of the wedding of Solomon and Shulamite is one of extravagant love. What is one way you can worship God this week in response to God's extravagant love for you?

Closing Prayer

Consider these prompts as you pray together for:

- A desire to seek God that is inspired by Shulamite's pursuit of Solomon
- The Holy Spirit to show us God's presence in our lives, like the cloud of presence in Exodus
- A renewed sense of the Bridegroom's extraordinary pursuit of us

Preparation

To prepare for the next group session:

1. **Read Song of Songs chapters 1–3** in their entirety one time before doing your homework.
2. Tackle the next three days of the Session 4 Personal Study.
3. Memorize this week's passage using the Beautiful Word Scripture memory coloring page. As a bonus, look up the Scripture memory passage in different translations and take note of the variations.
4. For next group's session, bring a treasured object that represents a person, a memory, or something that you love. (Think of a trinket from a fun trip, a family keepsake, a child's toy, a photograph, etc.)

Look on King Solomon wearing a crown, the crown with which his mother crowned him on the day of his wedding, the day his heart rejoiced.

—Song of Songs 3:11

SESSION

4

personal STUDY TIME

DIGGING INTO THE Beautiful WORD™ BIBLE STUDIES

SONG OF SONGS

A BREATHLESS SEARCH AND A BIG PARADE

Day 1

READ SONG OF SONGS 3:1–5

Chapter 3 of Song of Songs takes the reader on a turn. After all the excitement, anticipation, and longing in chapter 2, suddenly Shulamite cannot find Solomon. She searches all throughout the city and when she finds him, she will not let go of him again. The frantic search and the desperation in her voice show a level of preoccupation and fear reserved for that of a lover. When she finds him, she refuses to let go.

1. **Read verses 1–2.** Shulamite's search for Solomon evokes many emotions for the reader. Circle the three you most notice from the passage and add a few of your own in the blank spaces below.

frantic **desperate** **fearful** **anguished** **despondent**

nervous **wild** **searching** **panicked**

__________ __________ __________

2. We do not know, contextually, why Shulamite and Solomon have lost one another. Some scholars believe this is a dream sequence, a type of nightmare Shulamite has. Others, however, believe this may have actually happened and necessitated a physical search for him. Recall a time when you felt frantic (either emotionally or physically). Journal below about what that experience felt like.

3. **Read verse 3.** Shulamite asks the watchmen, who were likely patrolling the city walls, whether they have seen *"the one my heart loves."* Fill out the chart below, noting the elements of your faith you are still seeking and the ones you have found.

I Seek from God:	I Have Found in God:

4. "The one my heart loves" is a beautiful expression of tenderness and longing from Shulamite to Solomon. In the context of Solomon's kingship, her profession of love is particularly powerful. Reflect on that phrase in your own life below.

   Who is someone in your life that your heart loves? (Example: spouse, child, friend)

   What is a gift from God that your heart loves? (Example: sunshine, laughter)

   What is a part of your relationship with God that your heart particularly loves? (Example: God's peace, steadiness, joy)

"Have you seen the one my heart loves?"

Song of Songs 3:3

The difference in power and status between Solomon and Shulamite makes their desire for one another even more remarkable.

—Lisa Harper

5. **Read 3:4–5.** When Shulamite finds Solomon, the passage says she refuses to let him go. Picture them clinging to one another in relief. What emotions do you feel as you imagine yourself in Shulamite's shoes?

6. Verse 5 provides us with a refrain from chapter 2, imploring the daughters of Jerusalem not to awaken love before it so desires. Why do you think this refrain shows up here? How does Shulamite losing Solomon emphasize the power of love?

7. What is the emotional journey of Shulamite in these verses? Trace her experience below by filling in the chart.

Verse 1	
Verse 2	
Verse 3	
Verse 4	
Verse 5	

Day 2

READ SONG OF SONGS 3:6–8

After Shulamite and Solomon are separated from one another, the narrative rushes us forward to the beginning of their wedding. It is as if the moment Shulamite finds Solomon, the two realize they need to be together, always, and cannot wait to "seal the deal." The wedding scene begins with a parade, celebrating their love for one another, with Solomon on a carriage hoisted in the air by soldiers. The scene would have been extremely lavish. During this time period, Israel was extremely wealthy and powerful, so the celebration would have attracted important politicians and leaders from all over the Ancient Near East. Shulamite is suddenly the center of it all, watching Solomon begin to ascend the hill where she sits.

1. **Read verse 6.** Solomon is described as ascending toward her, up the mountain. His journey up the hill, carried by the most powerful soldiers in the land, mirrors an Israelite's ascent toward the temple. What do you think Shulamite is feeling as she sees Solomon ascend the hill?

2. **Read Psalm 121.** Psalm 121 is a Psalm of Ascent, describing the very journey of climbing the hill toward the temple. In Song of Songs, how does that journey mirror our own journey toward God?

The *soldiers* who carried Solomon were a type of *military force* created by his *father,* the mighty warrior *King David.*

3. Consider Shulamite's position in verse 6 compared with that of her description of her life before Solomon. (Remember, she was forced to work in the vineyards.) Fill in the chart.

Shulamite's Background	Shulamite's Current Status
Example: lower class	Example: upper class

Read verses 7–8. Solomon and the warriors are a show of strength and perseverance as they make their way toward Shulamite. Imagine Jesus pursuing you in the same way. What does it feel like to see Jesus climbing toward you like Solomon in this passage?

Write down the emotions this image evokes for you.

4. Notice the difference between Shulamite's vulnerability in verses 1–5 of this chapter (review those verses from yesterday if need be) and her positionality in verses 6–8. Compare and contrast those two images.

Verses 1–5	Verses 6–8
Example: alone	Example: surrounded by loved ones

5. Solomon, in these verses, comes up *"out of the wilderness"* (NKJV) much like God's people were guided up and out of the wilderness by His presence in the book of Exodus. **Read Exodus 15:17–18**, the song of Moses, and circle each word that reminds you of the scene in Song of Songs.

"You will bring them in and plant them on your own mountain,
the place, O Lord, which you have made for your abode,
the sanctuary, O Lord, which your hands have established.
The Lord will reign forever and ever" (ESV).

6. Write a prayer asking God to show you the ways He is moving toward you like Solomon in this passage.

Who is this coming up from the wilderness like a column of smoke?

Song of Songs 3:6

Day 3

READ SONG OF SONGS 3:9–11

Chapter 3 of Song of Songs ends with a description of Solomon's ornate carriage and crown. These last few verses remind the reader of his status as king of Israel, son of King David, and ruler over God's people at the height of their wealth and power. The carriage's materials and purple seat signal to the onlookers that no expense was spared for this royal wedding. The crown Solomon wears has been crafted by his mother, Bathsheba. Her life was marked by trauma and sorrow, but now she gets to have this beautiful redemptive moment as mother of the groom, signaling to the reader that her story has a redemptive arc.

1. **Read verses 9–10.** The royal carriage is described in detail in these verses. In the Bible, when the writers go to lengths to describe something physically, there is usually significance to that! Consider, for example, the Bible's descriptions of the temple in 1 Kings 5. In this passage, why do you think the carriage is described the way it is?

   What do these elements symbolize?

2. Imagine the carriage in your mind's eye and use the space below to draw your best rendering of Solomon on the carriage with the mighty men carrying him up the hill. No need to be a masterful artist! Just draw based on what you read and reflect on in the scene.

3. Verse 9 mentions that the carriage was made from the wood of Lebanon. In the Bible, the wood (or cedars) of Lebanon was a symbol of God's gifts and goodness to His people. What is a cedar of Lebanon in your own life?

Where do you see evidence of God's gifts and goodness?

4. **Read verse 11**, the last verse of this chapter. In this verse, we get to imagine the crown that Bathsheba makes for Solomon on his wedding day. Bathsheba was married to David after David illicitly summoned her to his quarters while her first husband was away on the battlefield. Scholars now acknowledge Bathsheba would have had no choice in this matter and was subject to a great trauma on that day. But this scene now gives Bathsheba a moment of redemption, in the spotlight, the day of her son's wedding. Take a moment to contemplate the life of Bathsheba. What do you think she was feeling in this moment as she laid the wreath on her son's head?

Look on King Solomon wearing a crown, the crown with which his mother crowned him on the day of his wedding, the day his heart rejoiced.

Song of Songs 3:11

In Hebrew, the word CROWN used in Song of Songs 3:11 means: *headdress, garland, wreath.*

5. The image of Solomon, crowned and ascending the hill to Shulamite, is one that shows us the extraordinary lengths he went to for his bride. When you contemplate the lengths God will go for you as your Bridegroom, how comfortable are you with this image? Circle where you are on the continuum.

❶ ← ❷ — ❸ — ❹ — ❺ — ❻ — ❼ — ❽ — ❾ → ❿

I do not feel worthy.	I am warming up to the idea.	I believe God loves me.	I am delighted in the Bridegroom.

6. As the king, Solomon truly could have pursued and wooed any woman, yet he chose Shulamite. When you imagine yourself being chosen and beloved by the Divine Bridegroom, Jesus, how do you feel? Write a prayer of gratitude to God.

7. Chapter 3 of Song of Songs progresses rapidly from a story of frantic searching to a wedding parade. Beside each part of the story, write three words that summarize the experience of Shulamite.

Search (3:1–3)	
Find (3:4–5)	
Parade (3:6–8)	
Ascend (3:9–11)	

Reflection

As you reflect on your personal study of Song of Songs 3, what are the **BEAUTIFUL WORDS** the Holy Spirit has been highlighting to you through this time? Write or draw them in the space below.

SESSION 5

THE PINNACLE OF PASSION

GROUP SESSION

SONG OF SONGS

Opening Group Activity (10-15 MINUTES)

WHAT YOU'LL NEED:

- ☑ Your treasured object you were instructed to bring last week
- ☑ If you forgot, just think about one that you would have brought and be prepared to describe it to the group.

1. Each participant is invited to spend one to two minutes sharing their treasured object and what it represents to them. Pass each object around as the person shares about it so that each participant can handle the object and behold its significance.
2. After spending time sharing each object, discuss these questions:

What did you notice about the objects? How did each participant describe their object?

What common themes did you discover when you heard about the person, memory, or something loved that each object was connected to?

Why do you think we keep treasures as representations of the sweet gifts in our lives?

SCRIPTURE COVERED IN THIS SESSION: SONG OF SONGS 4:1-5, 9, 16

Watch Session Five Video (34 MINUTES)

Leader, stream the video or play the DVD. As you watch, take notes on anything that stands out to you.

Song of Songs is tangible proof of the love we long for and points us to the perfect love of our Divine Bridegroom.

Chapter 4 is the pinnacle of their passion, which means it can feel more racy than other parts of this poetry.

Deep affection has an expulsive power. It is like the football player who barely notices the taunts of his teammates. Or it is like noise cancellation headphones for our hearts.

The veil Shulamite is wearing signifies this is her wedding day.

Hebraic poetry uses heightened language to describe Shulamite's beauty.

In the ancient world, Mount Gilead was 3,500 ft. high and a place where sheep and goats grazed until sunset . . . when the shepherds would call them down the mountain.

Shulamite having all her white teeth was significant as a beauty standard in the ancient world. Her cheeks described as pomegranates is a nod to the rosy color and the erotic connotation of pomegranates.

The description of Shulamite's breasts shows Solomon's deep desire for her and also reminds us that the Bible does not sanitize stories!

Verse 9 is a call to us to picture Jesus, our Divine Bridegroom, saying this to us.

The preoccupation of lovers for one another, and the last verse of invitation for Solomon to know her, biblically, shows us that sexual intimacy is good and beautiful within a marriage.

Sex and romantic love are signs of the goodness of God, pointing to God's desire to fully know us and love us.

Group Discussion Questions (30-45 MINUTES)

Leader Note: Spend time discussing the questions below together. As the leader, you can decide which questions to discuss, allowing flexibility for conversation and group interest.

1. Song of Songs can be read as tangible proof of God's love for us, like a symbol of His love. Think back to the object you brought to share with the group. What is one aspect of Song of Songs that feels like a symbol of God's love like your object?

2. **Read Song of Songs 4:1–7** together, assigning a different verse to each person. After each verse, pause and brainstorm what a modern-day equivalent of the description of Shulamite might be. For example, *"your hair is like a flock of goats"* might be communicated as "your hair is like a shampoo commercial" today. Get creative!

3. The descriptions of Shulamite are fairly racy, which can feel somewhat surprising for us to find in Scripture. What is your reaction to descriptions of Shulamite's appearance and breasts? Would you describe yourself as surprised, uncomfortable, completely fine with it? Reflect on that together.

4. Have one participant **read verse 9** slowly for the group. Picture Jesus saying this as your Divine Bridegroom in a wedding-type scene like chapter 4. What emotions does this evoke for you?

5. Sex is a sign for us, in our world, that points us to the joys God has for us. Sex and romantic intimacy reflects a love that is even better and more whole that can only come from Him. What is one thing you can do in your spiritual life to return to the early preoccupation and excitement in your relationship with Jesus?

6. As Solomon reaches his bride, it is as if everything else around him fades and he is fixated only on her. Search for the hymn "Turn Your Eyes Upon Jesus," and allow it to play for the group. Reflect together on the line "and the things of earth grow strangely dim" in light of this chapter.[13]

Closing Prayer

Consider these prompts as you pray together for:

- A return to our early preoccupation and love of Jesus like a new crush
- God to show us the depth of His love for us
- A heart to receive God's proclamation: "You have stolen my heart, my sister, my bride!"

Preparation

To prepare for the next group session:

1. **Read Song of Songs chapters 1–4** in their entirety one time before doing your homework.
2. Tackle the next three days of the Session 5 Personal Study.
3. Memorize this week's passage using the Beautiful Word Scripture memory coloring page. As a bonus, look up the Scripture memory passage in different translations and take note of the variations.
4. If you've agreed to bring something for the next session's Opening Group Activity, get it ready.

You have stolen my heart,
my sister, my bride; you
have stolen my heart with
one glance of your eyes,
with one jewel of
your necklace.

—Song of Songs 4:9

SESSION

5

personal STUDY TIME

DIGGING INTO THE

Beautiful WORD™ BIBLE STUDIES

SONG OF SONGS

THE PINNACLE OF PASSION

Day 1

READ SONG OF SONGS 4:1–7

Chapter 4 of Song of Songs opens as Solomon reaches his bride. In chapter 3, he and his mighty men were climbing the hill toward her, and now he has arrived and beholds his beloved. He is bursting with love, adoration, and excitement. He begins to describe her using heightened language common for Hebrew poetry of the time. Each description of her requires some cultural and historical context to fully understand. But once we do, we can see his love for her in each description.

1. **Verse 1** begins with: ***"How beautiful you are, my darling! Oh, how beautiful! Your eyes behind your veil are doves. Your hair is like a flock of goats descending from the hills of Gilead."*** Her eyes behind the veil indicate that this is her wedding day, as women typically wore veils only at weddings or on other special occasions. Make a list below of all the emotions associated with one's wedding day.

2. **Read verses 2–5.** Each ancient metaphor describing Shulamite layers on her beauty and Solomon's love for her. Fill out the following chart to list each metaphor given in this passage.

Shulamite's:	Are/Is Like:	Which Means:
Example: hair	Example: goats descending	Example: it's long and beautiful

There are seven similes used in this passage. Write one adjective below for each simile and then journal about how this reflects God's love for us.

-
-
-
-
-
-
-

3. Verse 6 describes the place where Solomon will go to find his beloved. The mountain of myrrh and the hill of incense are images that evoke something sacred. Myrrh and incense were used in ancient Israel in worshipful settings. How do these images invite us to see romantic love as a gift from God?

Read verse 7. Here, Solomon declares that Shulamite is altogether beautiful. We, as the reader, are invited to hear God speak that over us. Respond to each prompt below.

Something the beloved hears about herself in this passage: ______

Something you long for God to speak over you: ______

Something you know God is speaking over you: ______

The *tower of David* evoked in verse 4 is a nod to David's *military might* and is metaphorically an *adoration* of Shulamite's *long, beautiful* neck.

4. The ways Solomon speaks to Shulamite in this passage are very tender. If we are to use the voice of Solomon to hear from our Divine Bridegroom, then what does it look like to receive those affirmations from Jesus?

5. Write a prayer thanking God for the ways He gives us gifts of love on earth that point us to His divine love. Cite a few examples of that love in your own life.

Day 2

READ SONG OF SONGS 4:8–10

Solomon continues his adoration of his bride by calling her away from her home and her past. *"Come with me from Lebanon," "Amana," "Senir,"* and *"Hermon"* are all references to the northern, forested region of Lebanon (the same Lebanon from which the cedar wood came for Solomon's carriage). Solomon invites his new bride to leave her past behind and embark on this new journey of marriage with him. It is as if they have reached the pinnacle of their wedding celebration and Solomon can now declare Shulamite as his wife and usher her into her new life with him.

1. Solomon begins verse 8 by inviting Shulamite to come with him. In the left-hand column, list each place or thing she is invited to leave behind. In the right-hand column, write down two to three emotions or experiences that element might symbolize.

Come Away From:	Which Means:
Example: Lebanon	Example: a new start

The language in verse 8 connotes a treacherous landscape and an invitation away from difficulty and harm in Shulamite's old life. In the peaks and valleys of the mountain landscape below, write down aspects of your own life that God is calling you away from.

The *ancient mount of Amana* is likely referring to a mountain range that *borders* modern-day *Lebanon* and *Syria*.[14]

2. **Read verse 9.** The refrain *"my sister, my bride"* shows up again in this verse. Here, Solomon tells Shulamite that she has stolen his heart. Imagine God declaring to you that you have stolen His heart. Now **reread verse 9** and fill in the blanks below.

   The word/phrase that feels most comforting in this verse is:

   The word/phrase that feels hardest to believe in this verse is:

   I think that is because:

3. **Verse 10** goes on to hear Solomon say, *"How delightful is your love, my sister, my bride! How much more pleasing is your love than wine, and the fragrance of your perfume more than any spice!"* Her love is more pleasing than wine, perfume, and spices. If you were to declare your love to someone, what three things would you say their love is more pleasing than? (Example: chocolate, sunshine, tacos)

4. Verses 8–10 move the story from a treacherous place (the mountains of Lebanon) to pure affection and delight. Reread all three verses and notice how the emotional tone shifts. If God were inviting you out of those mountains, where would you find yourself within these verses? Circle which one you relate to most and journal about why.

   Frightened, stuck (verse 8)

   Moving toward God (in verse 9)

   Fully basking in God's love (in verse 10)

5. Look back at question 2 and the things you wrote down that God is calling you away from. Now, based on verses 9–10 of this chapter, write down a few things that God is calling you *toward.*

6. Rewrite verse 10 in your own words as though Jesus is speaking directly to you. Pray through that verse, asking God to release you from the treacherous mountains in your own life.

Day 3

READ SONG OF SONGS 4:11–16

Chapter 4 culminates in a celebration of the love between Solomon and Shulamite. Solomon describes her beauty in ways that show his delight in her sexuality, which they now enjoy with one another after their marriage ceremony. The main metaphor Solomon now employs is that of a garden. He lists the fruits and spices in her garden, many of them having an erotic connotation, as he celebrates her beauty. The passage ends with Shulamite inviting Solomon into her garden as they consummate their marriage.

1. **Read verse 11.** In the Bible, milk and honey signify richness and abundance. The land of Israel, promised to God's people, is often described throughout Scripture as "the land flowing with milk and honey." Why do you think Solomon uses this phrase when describing Shulamite?

2. **Verse 12** says, *"You are a garden locked up, my sister, my bride; you are a spring enclosed, a sealed fountain."* This metaphor is likely referring to her virginity. She is a garden, but Solomon has not yet gone into the garden. He has long awaited this day and is anticipating knowing her fully and completely. Think back to Solomon and Shulamite's journey in their relationship. What emotions might be coming up for the two of them in this moment?

3. **Read verses 13 and 14.** Here, Solomon describes all the fruits and spices in Shulamite's garden. He continues his celebration of her and his excitement to become one with her. He is entirely preoccupied with Shulamite! Romantic relationships and sexual intimacy are gifts from God that point to God's goodness. Brainstorm other parts of life that also point to God's goodness below. (Example: sunsets)

-
-
-
-

4. Many of the words Solomon uses in this passage evoke the sweetness of their relationship. What sweetness does your relationship with God bring to you?

   How does your relationship with God nourish your soul?

5. **Read verse 15.** Water imagery in Scripture signifies life. Jesus, for example, promises living water in John 7 to those who follow Him. How has your relationship with God proven to be a source of living water for you? Journal about one example below.

Your lips drop sweetness as the honeycomb, my bride; milk and honey are under your tongue.

Song of Songs 4:11

Richard Hess tells us that Solomon calling Shulamite *"my sister, my bride"* indicates that he not only sees her as his legal *wife* but also as his closest *peer* and *friend*.[15]

6. **Verse 16** says:

   Awake, north wind,
   and come, south wind!
   Blow on my garden,
   that its fragrance may spread everywhere.
   Let my beloved come into his garden
   and taste its choice fruits.

   Circle each instance of heightened language (metaphor, hyperbole, personification, etc.) in the verse above. Put a star next to the one that most resonates with you.

7. Verse 16 is Shulamite's response to Solomon. She invites him into her garden, meaning she is now saying that she and Solomon are fully intimate and know one another wholly. Write a prayer thanking God for the gift of romantic relationships and sexuality, as they point us to God's goodness.

Reflection

As you reflect on your personal study of Song of Songs 4, what are the **BEAUTIFUL WORDS** the Holy Spirit has been highlighting to you through this time? Write or draw them in the space below.

SESSION 6

WHEN DELIGHT TURNS TO DRUDGERY

GROUP SESSION

SONG OF SONGS

Opening Group Activity (10-15 MINUTES)

WHAT YOU'LL NEED:

- ☑ A posterboard or whiteboard
- ☑ Pens or dry-erase markers

1. Have one participant create two columns on the board. The first should say "delight" and the second should say "drudgery." That participant will record the group's responses.
2. Each participant is invited to brainstorm blessings in their lives or in the lives of those around them. Shout out each answer and write them all on the board under "delight." Answers might include: a loving spouse, wonderful children, getting an education, or a job that is meaningful.
3. Each participant is then invited to brainstorm how those "delights" might turn to drudgery in their lives or in the lives of those around them. Write those responses on the board under "drudgery." Answers might include: a spouse who keeps forgetting to get the mail, children always fighting with each other, having to do homework, or an irritating coworker.
4. After spending time creating those lists, discuss these questions:

    What do you notice about these two columns? Does anything stand out to you from this exercise?

    What delight or drudgery do you most relate to? Why?

    Why do you think the blessings/delights in our lives can so quickly turn to drudgery? How can we actively safeguard against this?

SCRIPTURE COVERED IN THIS SESSION: SONG OF SONGS 5:2-8, 10-16; JOSHUA 3:7-13; 4:21-24

Watch Session Six Video (34 MINUTES)

Leader, stream the video or play the DVD. As you watch, take notes on anything that stands out to you.

The move from delight to drudgery, from devoted to undisciplined, can be very short in our lives.

Chapter 5 starts with Shulamite rebuffing Solomon's advances.

When Shulamite changes her mind, Solomon is gone. So, she searches for him but does not find him for a long time.

While searching for Solomon, the watchmen abuse her and take her cloak.

Shulamite, in verse 10, begins to recount everything she loves about Solomon when she can't find him.

The taking of *Shulamite's cloak* is a nod to the story of Joseph in Genesis. *Joseph's cloak* is taken twice in his story in a way that violates him and his identity.

- In Joshua chapter 3, God calls the Israelites to cross the Jordan River by putting their feet in the water, in faith. Relational intimacy is risky!

- God's people are called to make a stone monument to commemorate their crossing the Jordan. Why? To remember God's faithfulness.

- Like the Israelites making a monument, Shulamite begins to recount Solomon's goodness as a spouse when she cannot find him. She remembers his love and turns back to delight.

- If we feel distant from God, we can recall His blessings in our lives, much like Shulamite recalls Solomon's love.

Group Discussion Questions (30–45 MINUTES)

Leader Note: Spend time discussing the questions below together. As the leader, you can decide which questions to discuss, allowing flexibility for conversation and group interest.

1. Lisa told her story of going from worshiping in the car to throwing her daughter Missy's biscuit out the window! What is a story that comes to mind where you went from delight to drudgery really quickly? Has that ever happened to you with God?

2. Shulamite goes searching for Solomon but instead encounters the watchmen, who beat her and take her cloak. How do you think she is feeling in such a vulnerable position in that moment? Make a list of her emotions together.

3. **Read Song of Songs 5:10–16** together. When Shulamite cannot find Solomon, this is when she begins to recount everything that she loves about him. After you've read those verses together, choose one description that stands out to you and share with the group why it does. If you were to choose one aspect of God's character to recount, what would it be and why?

4. In the story of God's people crossing the Jordan, the Israelites are asked to step into the water before God miraculously dries it up. What would it look like for you to step into the metaphorical water in faith, courageously, trusting God to act?

5. The Israelites commemorate God's miracle with a monument of stones. They do this to remember God's faithfulness to them. What is something in your life that you can point to that reminds you of God's faithfulness?

6. We are encouraged to recount God's blessings when we feel distant from Him. Make a list of blessings as a group and then pray over them together, thanking God for each one.

Closing Prayer

Consider these prompts as you pray together for:

- A commitment to safeguard our hearts against our delight turning to drudgery
- The Holy Spirit to call to mind our blessings from God, to recount them again and again
- The courage to pursue relational intimacy with God

Preparation

To prepare for the next group session:

1. **Read Song of Songs chapters 1–6** in their entirety one time before doing your homework.
2. Tackle the next three days of the Session 6 Personal Study.
3. Memorize this week's passage using the Beautiful Word Scripture memory coloring page. As a bonus, look up the Scripture memory passage in different translations and take note of the variations.
4. For the next group's session, bring a stone or rock that is smooth enough to write on. Find one in your backyard or somewhere in nature. If you can't find one, simply cut a piece of paper into the shape of a stone and bring that!

Daughters of Jerusalem,

I charge you—if you find my beloved,
what will you tell him?
Tell him I am faint with love.

—Song of Songs 5:8

SESSION

6

personal STUDY TIME

DIGGING INTO THE Beautiful WORD™ BIBLE STUDIES

SONG OF SONGS

WHEN DELIGHT TURNS TO DRUDGERY

Day 1

READ SONG OF SONGS 5:1–8

Chapter 5 of Song of Songs opens with Solomon's continued love and desire for Shulamite. He approaches her door and wants to come in. In other words, Solomon desires her, intimately, and shows up knocking. Their honeymoon has happened, they are back at home, and daily married life is now settling in. In the ancient world, because Solomon was royalty, Shulamite would have had her own chambers, which is why he is knocking on her door in order to have an intimate moment with her. However, in verse 3, she bemoans the fact that she is all ready for bed. Her feet are washed and she is no longer wearing her robe. Culturally, washing one's feet is like our modern version of winding down for the evening and brushing our teeth. Wearing sandals meant feet got very dirty and dusty, so foot washing was a hygienic practice at the end of the day. Shulamite is "in for the night" and hesitates when Solomon suddenly comes to call.

Verses 4–8 of chapter 5 describe Shulamite's moment of regret when she realizes Solomon is gone. Much like earlier in the poem, Shulamite looks for Solomon. She goes through the streets, calling for him, but she does not find him. In the passage, the watchmen beat her and take her cloak. Some scholars believe this is a dream sequence but others say this likely could have happened. Culturally, in the Ancient Near East, for a woman to be out at night, wandering unaccompanied, would have been considered shameful. So, it is within the realm of possibility that this actually did happen to her. The stripping of her cloak, a nod to the story of Joseph in the book of Genesis, signifies a loss of her dignity and protection. This passage ends with her declaration to the daughters of Jerusalem that she is faint with love for him.

1. In **verse 1**, Solomon says:

    I have come into my garden, my sister, my bride;
    I have gathered my myrrh with my spice.
    I have eaten my honeycomb and my honey;
    I have drunk my wine and my milk.

    And then the chorus of friends echoes: ***"Eat, friends, and drink; drink your fill of love."***

    Slowly read through verse 1 and highlight or circle every word/phrase that connotes intimacy with Shulamite.

2. **Read verses 2–3.** Find the ways this passage communicates Solomon's desire and note them in the left-hand column. Then, find the ways this passage communicates Shulamite's hesitancy and note them in the right-hand column.

Desire	Hesitancy

3. Notice in verse 3 how Shulamite gives two reasons why she does not want to be intimate with Solomon. What are the reasons that tend to pop up for you when you are resisting spiritual intimacy with Jesus? Write them below on the lines and then write a prayer below each, asking God to quiet those hesitancies. (Examples: busyness, anxiety, feeling disconnected)

- ____________________

- ____________________

- ____________________

Foot washing was multi-faceted in the ancient world. It could serve as a daily *hygiene* practice, a religious *ritual*, or a practice of *hospitality*. In Shulamite's case, she was washing her feet as a daily hygienic practice.

I have *taken off* my robe— must I *put it on* again? I have *washed* my feet— must I *soil* them again?

Song of Songs 5:3

4. **Read verses 4–5.** Solomon is at her gate and her hesitation turns into anticipation. Recall her hesitation in verse 3 (she had already washed her feet and taken off her robe). If you were in her shoes, what do you think would have changed for you from verse 3 to verses 4–5?

   Why do you think she was suddenly anticipatory?

5. **Verse 6** says,

   I opened for my beloved, but my beloved had left; he was gone. My heart sank at his departure. I looked for him but did not find him. I called him but he did not answer.

   Circle all the verbs in this verse. Which one feels the weightiest to you?

   What does your chosen verb reveal about the nature of relational longing?

6. Shulamite departs to look for Solomon, mirroring her search in chapter 3. Go back and **reread Song of Songs 3:1–5** and compare those verses to 5:7–8 using the Venn diagram.

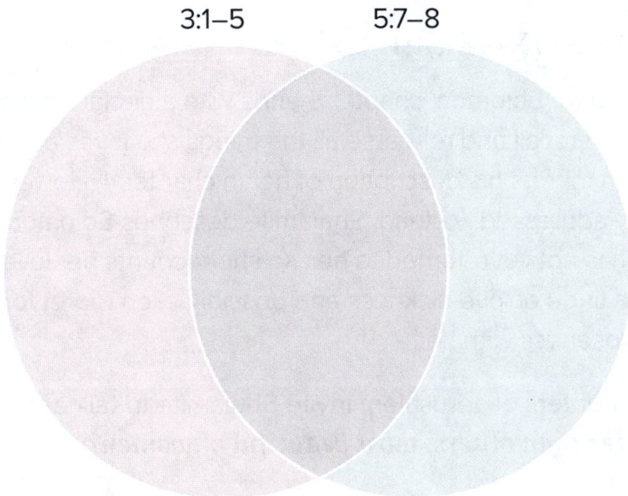

7. By **verse 8**, Shulamite describes herself as *"faint with love."* She is desperate for Solomon after she initially rebuffs him earlier. Journal in the following space about a time you experienced some drudgery in your relationship with God but later desired Him in a deeper way.

8. *"If you find my beloved, what will you tell him?"* is the question Shulamite ends with in this passage. If you were speaking to someone about God, how would you fill in this blank?

   If you find Him, tell Him ______________________________
   ____
   ____.

   What would you like to tell God? Write a prayer below.

Day 2

READ SONG OF SONGS 5:9–16

After Shulamite's search for Solomon, chapter 5 ends with a declaration of her love for him. Shulamite begins to recall and rehearse all the things she loves about Solomon. This description of Solomon mirrors his description of her in chapter 4. However, this time, the beloved is not directly addressed. Instead, Shulamite describes Solomon to the daughters of Jerusalem. Solomon has not yet returned to her, so she recounts her love for him to others. The reader can hear a tinge of love-sickness and possibly even regret for rebuffing his previous attempt at closeness with her.

1. **In verse 9**, the daughters of Jerusalem invite Shulamite to talk about Solomon: ***"How is your beloved better than others, most beautiful of women?"***

   "How is your beloved better than others, that you so charge us?"

   If you were to rewrite their questions in modern language, what would you say?

2. **Read verses 10–16** slowly. Choose one descriptor you resonate with the most and draw it below.

   Then, describe in one sentence why that metaphor is so beautiful to you.

3. Solomon is a king, and many of Shulamite's descriptions remind us of his incredible wealth, power, and stature. List every element of her description that points us toward his wealth and power.

Descriptor	This Points to Royalty Because:
Example: gold	Example: kings wear gold crowns

4. Shulamite, in this passage, is calling to mind everything she loves about Solomon. She does this right after rebuffing his advances and falling into relational monotony. If you were to call to mind the things you love about God, what would be the top three things you would list? (Examples: God's goodness, His love, His faithfulness)

-
-
-

5. Take each element you listed in the previous question and create a metaphor from that attribute of God. For example, "God's goodness is like the purity of a child" or "God's love is like a gentle breeze on a warm day."

-
-
-

In 5:13, Shulamite says Solomon's *"lips are like lilies dripping with myrrh."* Myrrh was an incredibly expensive spice in the ancient world, connoting value and worth.

This is my *beloved,* this is my *friend,* daughters of Jerusalem.

Song of Songs 5:16b

6. This chapter ends with Shulamite declaring, ***"His mouth is sweetness itself; he is altogether lovely. This is my beloved, this is my friend, daughters of Jerusalem."***

   What do you think is the significance of Shulamite calling Solomon not only her beloved but also her friend?

7. Solomon was the king of Israel, and Shulamite, from a much lower station, was able to call him friend. Likewise, Jesus declares that we get to call Him friend. How does that declaration reveal the intimacy we are invited into in relationship with Jesus?

Day 3

READ SONG OF SONGS 6:1–9

Chapter 6 begins with a question from the daughters of Jerusalem: ***"Where has your beloved gone?"*** This time, Shulamite knows the answer. He has gone down to his garden. This signals to the reader that we are entering a time of daily life and marriage in Solomon and Shulamite's relationship. Shulamite knows where Solomon is and continues to admire him and declare that they belong to each other. Starting in verse 4, Solomon speaks. His declarations of love for Shulamite mirror his same declaration in chapter 4. He ends by declaring Shulamite to be unique. He mentions other queens and concubines, but she is the one who stands out amongst them all. The Bible tells us in 1 Kings that Solomon begins to accumulate for himself many wives and concubines as his wealth and power grow. This ultimately leads to his downfall. But in this poetry, we can see an acknowledgment that Shulamite is set apart from the rest.

In chapter 6, the daughters of Jerusalem ask Shulamite where her beloved has gone, so that they can go searching with her. The theme of searching for her beloved echoes throughout Song of Songs. Look back at **Song of Songs 3:1–4; 5:2–7; and 6:2-3, 11–12**.

Fill in the chart below, tracing where Shulamite seeks and finds her beloved throughout Song of Songs, and identify the common themes that show in these "seeking" passages.

Where Shulamite seeks	
Where Shulamite finds	
Themes in the searching	

1. **Read Song of Songs 6:4–9.** Choose one image for love from these verses and sketch it below (no need to be a perfect artist!). Then, write a prayer beneath it, asking God to reveal to you the ways He finds you lovely.

2. Solomon's imagery in these verses mirrors that in **chapter 4, verses 1–7**. Reread those verses and then write down every image or metaphor you find that is the same or similar to those in **verses 4–9** of chapter 6.

3. In verses 8–9, Solomon says Shulamite is set apart from all other wives and concubines. **Read 1 Kings 11:1–4.** How does this passage inform the way Solomon talks about Shulamite in Song of Songs?

4. Solomon compares Shulamite's beauty to that of Jerusalem and Tirzah. Jerusalem was the epicenter of the land of Israel, home to Solomon's palace and, more importantly, God's temple. Tirzah was a city-center in the north in Israel, known for its beauty. Rewrite verse 4 in modern-day language. What cities or locations would you use to describe someone's beauty?

5. Shulamite, in this passage, is the chosen one among many. Likewise, God calls us chosen. We are set apart, beloved by Him. Considering these parallels, fill out the following chart.

Shulamite Is Chosen Because:	God Chooses Us Because:

I am my beloved's and my beloved is mine; he browses among the lilies.

Song of Songs 6:3

Reflection

As you reflect on your personal study of Song of Songs 5–6, what are the **BEAUTIFUL WORDS** the Holy Spirit has been highlighting to you through this time? Write or draw them in the space below.

SESSION 7

SEALED WITH SECURITY

GROUP SESSION

SONG OF SONGS

Opening Group Activity (10–15 MINUTES)

WHAT YOU'LL NEED:

- ☑ Each participant should have a stone that they were asked to bring last week
- ☑ A permanent marker for each participant

1. Participants are invited, in one to two minutes of silence, to contemplate the question, "What made me first fall in love with Jesus?"
2. Each participant will take another minute to write down a word or phrase that describes their answer to that question. It could be an attribute of God, a moment in time, or a blessing in their life.
3. Go around the group and allow each participant to share their word or phrase and what it describes. As each participant shares, they should place their stone in the center of the group, stacking the stones as the group describes their answers. (Don't stack them somewhere too precarious . . . you can always head outside if need be!)
4. At the end of the time of sharing, there should be a makeshift monument that recounts each participant's gratitude to God and blessings from the Lord.
5. After the monument is complete, discuss these questions:

   What story or blessing most resonated with you and why?

   What are two to three emotions you are feeling as you see this pile of stones and remember the goodness of God?

   Why do you think the practice of recounting God's goodness can help us feel close to God when He feels distant?

SCRIPTURE COVERED IN THIS SESSION: SONG OF SONGS 7:7–9; 8:5–10; LUKE 8:1–3; EPHESIANS 3:14–19

Watch Session Seven Video (38 MINUTES)

Leader, stream the video or play the DVD. As you watch, take notes on anything that stands out to you.

- In a secure, whole relationship, commitment and contentment merge into one.

- Chapters 6 and 7 of Song of Songs describe the dailiness of life in marriage.

- The brothers' voices in chapter 8 call into question Shulamite's purity, but she responds with confidence and security that her "breasts are like towers."

- Mary Magdalene (from Magdala, meaning "tower") is another example of a beautiful blend of humility and confidence as she preaches the resurrection.

- Song of Songs 8:6–7 culminates the entire book by declaring the love of Shulamite and Solomon cannot be quenched or thwarted. They are secure in their relationship.

The Septuagint is a Greek translation of the Hebrew Scriptures.

Agape: love, when translated into the Greek in the Septuagint seen in Song of Songs 8:6–7

The word ***agape*** is used in the story of Jesus asking Peter, "Do you love me?" three times (John 21:15–17). But the third time, Jesus switches to the word *phileo*, meaning "friendship love."

Love takes the *sting* out of *duty*.[16]

—Dr. Robertson McQuilkin

The romantic love of Song of Songs is not the main takeaway. The main takeaway is God's *agape* love for us.

Much like orphans settling for small bits of attention, we settle in the same way with God because we often struggle to see ourselves as God's children.

Are there corners of our hearts that are still uncomfortable with God calling us beloved?

Group Discussion Questions (30-45 MINUTES)

Leader Note: Spend time discussing the questions below together. As the leader, you can decide which questions to discuss, allowing flexibility for conversation and group interest.

1. Song of Songs 6–7 describes the dailiness of life. Even in the moments when our faith doesn't feel like "fireworks," how can we know that God is still with us?

2. **Read Song of Songs 8:8–12.** Shulamite's response to her brothers is one of confidence and security. She is like a mother in the house of God. She protects, nurtures, and provides. Go around the group and name one woman in your life who has been a spiritual mother to you or to your faith community. How do you see God using women in your life for your spiritual growth and formation?

3. Ask someone in the group to read the entirety of **John chapter 20**. Once you have listened to the story, brainstorm as a group all the ways Mary lives up to her Magdala (tower) heritage. (Remember: Towers symbolized strength, confidence, and security in the ancient world.)

4. Song of Songs 8:6–7 is the culmination of the entire book of Song of Songs. Choose a metaphor for unending love that resonates with you the most, and tell the group why.

5. The word love in verses 6–7 is translated as *agape* in the Septuagint. *Agape*, in the Greek, refers to unconditional or sacrificial love. What does it look like in your life for you to sacrifice for others as a sign of love? How has God shown *agape* love to you?

6. The story of the group of orphans learning to perform for love and attention is a powerful picture of the ways we feel the need to perform for God. We often can struggle or feel uncomfortable with God calling us beloved. Create a T-chart as a group. In the left-hand column, write down the ways each of you sees yourself as orphans considering God's love. In the right-hand column, write down the ways each of you sees yourself as fully secure children of God. Pray over each list.

Closing Prayer

Consider these prompts as you pray together for:

- A confident security in your faith, the way Shulamite responds to her brothers
- A love for God that endures in both commitment and contentment
- A willingness to accept God's *agape* love

Preparation

To prepare for the next group session:

1. **Read Song of Songs chapters 1–8** in their entirety one time before doing your homework.
2. Tackle the next three days of the Session 7 Personal Study.
3. Memorize this week's passage using the Beautiful Word Scripture memory coloring page. As a bonus, look up the Scripture memory passage in different translations and take note of the variations.

Many *waters* cannot quench *love*;
rivers cannot sweep it away. If one were to give all the wealth
of one's house for *love*, it would be utterly scorned.

—Song of Songs 8:7

SESSION

7

personal STUDY TIME

DIGGING INTO THE

Beautiful WORD™ BIBLE STUDIES

SONG OF SONGS

SEALED WITH SECURITY

Day 1

MOUNT CARMEL is known in the Bible as the place where **ELIJAH** had his famous **SHOWDOWN** with the **FALSE GOD** Ba'al in 1 Kings 18.

READ SONG OF SONGS 6:10–7:9

The daughters of Jerusalem reenter the scene and ask, ***"Who is this that appears like the dawn?"*** In response, Solomon continues to narrate his love for Shulamite all the way through chapter 7, verse 9. He describes going down to the valley of nut trees but that his desire is to be with Shulamite. In chapter 7, he, once again, praises her beauty. Many of the metaphors are very similar to earlier chapters. However, some of the images used seem to suggest a progression of time. For example, her breasts are described as clusters of fruit. And Solomon describes her eyes in new and different ways. The descriptions invite the reader to contemplate a deepening of love. These descriptions are not the beginnings of a crush. Now, they are born of deep admiration, friendship, and relational longevity.

1. **Read verse 10**. Make a list below of words that describe Shulamite's portrayal in Song of Songs and traits in your own life that shine like the dawn. Circle the three that resonate with you the most.

2. **Read verses 11–13.** Solomon goes down to the valley to see if the vines are budding. In other words, the passage is telling us it is now springtime. In the context of love and relationships, list five to seven things springtime might represent. Then, journal about a time in your relationship with God that felt like springtime.

3. **Chapter 7, verses 1–9** are a continuation of Solomon's admiration of Shulamite. Read them slowly and notice any different or new metaphors Solomon uses. Write the new ones you encounter below and then a brief description of what you think they mean.

New Metaphor	New Meaning

4. Solomon utilizes many images to highlight Shulamite's strength and beauty. In the Venn diagram below, list each image under the characteristic it highlights. Are there any you think highlight both?

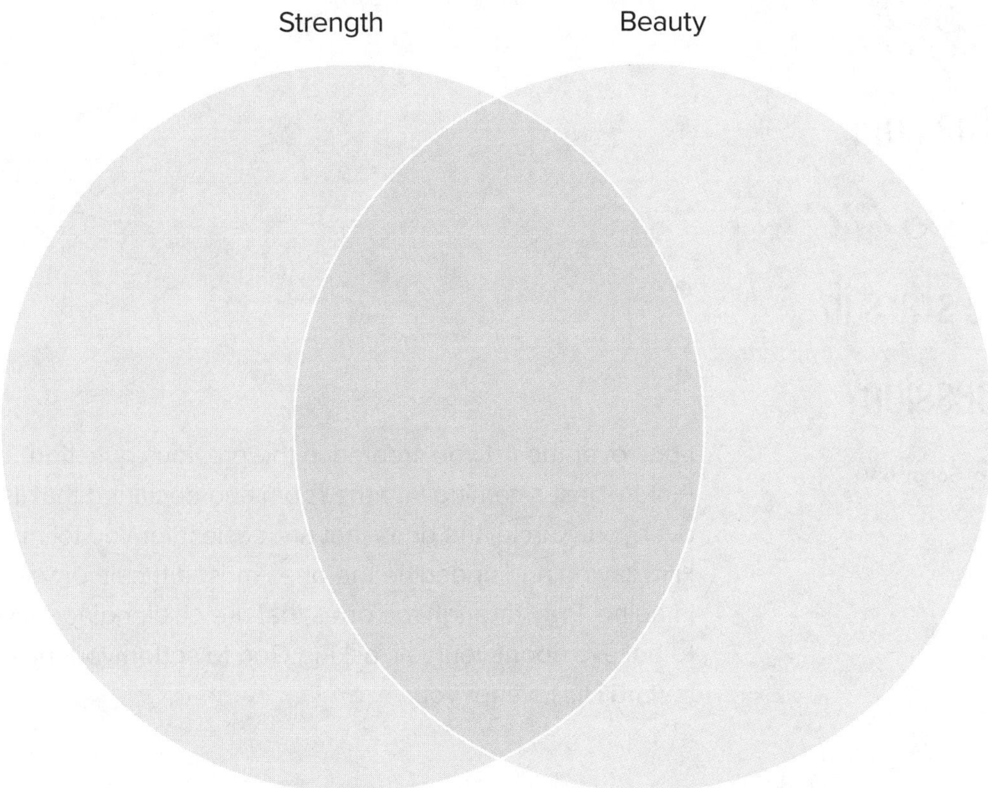

5. Solomon mentions five locations in this passage: Mount Carmel, Damascus, Lebanon, Bath-rabbim, and Heshbon. These sites are all over the land of Israel. Why do you think this is significant?

What does it say about his love for her?

Who is this that *appears* like the dawn, *fair* as the moon, *bright* as the sun, *majestic* as the stars in procession?

Song of Songs 6:10

6. Many passages in Song of Songs, including this one, are full of rich language admiring each beloved. If God were to make a list for you, what do you think He would include? Write that list below.

-
-
-
-
-

7. Look over the list you created in the previous question. Picture Jesus coming into the room and declaring that list over you. Circle the ones that are easiest for you to imagine Him saying and underline the ones most difficult for you to imagine. Pray through the ones that are challenging for you to believe about yourself, asking God to soften your heart toward His love for you.

Day 2

READ SONG OF SONGS 7:10–8:5

Chapter 7 closes with a return to Shulamite's voice. She reiterates her earlier proclamation that she belongs to Solomon and Solomon belongs to her. In response to his admiration and love, she invites him away for the weekend. ***"Come, my beloved, let us go to the countryside, let us spend the night in the villages,"*** she says in verse 11. Her invitation to go to the vineyards to see if they have budded indicates that it is springtime. Their love has grown and they are in a new, fresh season in their relationship. Much like pomegranates, the mandrake, mentioned in verse 13, was considered erotic in the ancient world, and its scent was reminiscent of fertility. So, Shulamite is communicating to Solomon that their love is renewed.

Chapter 8 opens with a poetic declaration of emotional intimacy. Shulamite says she wishes Solomon were like a brother. Nothing untoward is going on here. In this ancient context, this likely means she could be more outwardly affectionate toward him in public if he were part of her immediate family, as that was more culturally acceptable. There is also a certain peer-to-peer relational dynamic with a sibling that portrays emotional intimacy that Shulamite is relaxing into in this verse. In chapter 8, Shulamite and Solomon have been married for a long time and they are fully comfortable with one another and still love one another deeply. Verse 5 asks, ***"Who is this coming up from the wilderness?"*** This is another nod to God bringing the Israelites up out of the wilderness and into the promised land. The theme throughout this passage continues to be relational closeness, both between Solomon and Shulamite, and between God and His people.

1. **Read through verses 7:10–13** slowly. Shulamite begins this passage by declaring, ***"I belong to my beloved, and his desire is for me."*** Use the chart to describe what it feels like to belong with another person and what it feels like to belong with God.

Belonging with Another Feels Like:	Belonging with God Feels Like:

I belong to my beloved, and his desire is for me.

Song of Songs 7:10

2. Verses 7:11–12 follow the poetical structure listed below. Fill in the blanks to turn the poetry toward God.

   Come, God, let us go to ______________________.

   There I want to show You ______________________.

   May You find delight in ______________________.

3. The invitation to come away with one's beloved echoes throughout Song of Songs. On the path below, draw or write out where you believe God is inviting you to journey with Him.

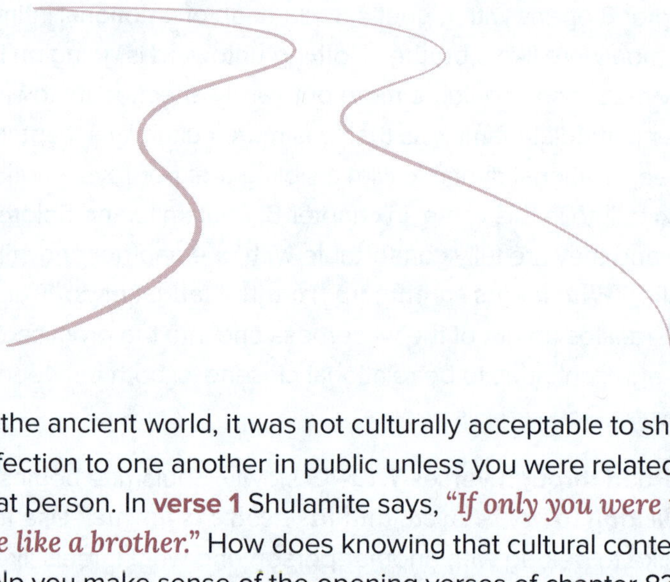

4. In the ancient world, it was not culturally acceptable to show affection to one another in public unless you were related to that person. In **verse 1** Shulamite says, ***"If only you were to me like a brother."*** How does knowing that cultural context help you make sense of the opening verses of chapter 8?

5. **In verse 8:2**, Shulamite expresses a desire to bring Solomon to her mother's house. Make a list of the emotions, pictures, and feelings that arise when picturing the warmth of a mother's house. What do you think it says about Shulamite and Solomon's relationship that she wants to take him there?

6. **Read Song of Songs 8:3 and Song of Songs 2:6.** What do you notice? Knowing chapter 8 represents the longevity of their marriage and chapter 2 represents young love, what do these mirroring verses communicate about their love?

7. **Read verses 4–5.** In the Bible, coming up from the wilderness symbolizes coming out of a time of trial and difficulty. In the Old Testament, God brought His people up out of the wilderness and into the promised land. What do you think it means, then, for Shulamite and Solomon to come up out of the wilderness as a couple?

8. Think about your own faith journey. Circle where you are on the continuum.

❶ ← ❷ — ❸ — ❹ — ❺ — ❻ — ❼ — ❽ — ❾ → ❿

Before the wilderness (I am newly Christian or seeing my faith anew.)	In the wilderness (This is a time of trials and struggle.)	Coming out of the wilderness (God is bringing me out of a time of struggle in my faith.)

Day 3

READ SONG OF SONGS 8:6–14

Verses 6 and 7 are the true pinnacle of the entirety of the Song of Songs as they are the final declaration of Solomon and Shulamite's, unending love for one another. Their love is like a seal over their hearts and is as strong as death. Their love is described as a burning flame. Throughout the New Testament, the image of a flame usually points to the Holy Spirit. The Holy Spirit is evidence of God's love for us. Their love is also described as a love that cannot be quenched by the waters. In the ancient world, the waters symbolized chaos. So, in other words, the love between Solomon and Shulamite can endure chaos. Finally, their love is said to be more valuable than the wealthiest home. Considering Solomon's net worth, that is quite the statement! All these declarations point to the reality that Solomon and Shulamite not only love each other but their love is *enduring.*

Song of Songs ends with an interesting question-and-answer sequence. The brothers of Shulamite, in verses 8–9, question her purity when she got married. Was she a wall? (Did she remain sexually pure before her wedding?) Or was she a door? (Did she allow men to engage with her?) Shulamite answers with confidence that she is a wall. She also declares her breasts to be like towers. In other words, she very securely declares that she is a powerful mother-type figure. She knows who she is and she is confident in her marriage. This book ends with her humble, yet confident, declaration of her identity. Her progression from young, frantic maiden to older, confident woman is a beautiful journey to punctuate the end of this poem.

1. **Verses 6–7** employ many pictures of what it means for love to be enduring. Circle each picture you see of their love in these verses.

Place me like a seal over your heart,
like a seal on your arm;
for love is as strong as death,
its jealousy unyielding as the grave.
It burns like blazing fire,
like a mighty flame.
Many waters cannot quench love;
rivers cannot sweep it away.
If one were to give
all the wealth of one's house for love,
it would be utterly scorned.

2. This passage employs many images of Solomon and Shulamite's enduring love. Fill in the blanks below to reflect on the ways you see God's enduring love in your life.

God's love for me is like

____.

Because of this, I know

____.

God's love for me is like

____.

So, I can feel assured because

____.

God's love for me is like

____.

Therefore, I know that I am

____.

3. When the Hebrew word for love is translated into Greek, that Greek word here is *agape*, meaning a love that is unconditional. Think back over the entirety of the Song of Songs. What are three examples you can think of when Solomon and Shulamite show unconditional love to one another? List them below.

-
-
-

Many *waters* *cannot* *quench* love; *rivers* *cannot* *sweep* it away.

Song of Songs 8:7a

Shulamite describes her breasts as towers in verse 10. Towers, in the Bible, signify strength and power.

4. **Read verses 8–9.** These verses are the moment of questioning Shulamite's brothers have regarding her status when she married Solomon. Did she remain pure before marriage or did she not?

In the Ancient Near East, Shulamite's brothers would have been her guardians if her father could not fulfill that duty. Considering this, why do you think they ask this question in the poem?

5. Shulamite's response in verses 10–12 is one of confidence in herself and in her value. Compare and contrast her declaration in 8:10–12 with her early statements about herself in chapter 1:5–6.

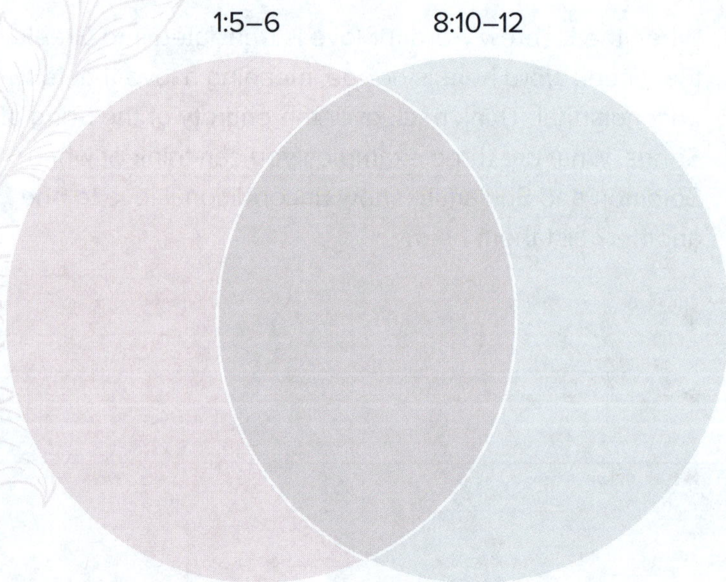

6. Shulamite says, *"My own vineyard is mine to give"* (verse 12), when describing her virginity. Her statement demonstrates confidence, much like her description of herself as a tower. When you think about your own faith, how have you grown in confidence in your identity in Christ? Journal about one example.

7. **Read verses 13 and 14.** These final verses of Song of Songs are a reflection of the poetry as a whole. What is one theme you notice in these verses that you have seen in prior passages throughout this study?

8. What does Song of Songs communicate about being fully seen, loved, and known?

Write a prayer asking God to reveal to you the ways He loves you, sees you, and knows you wholly.

Reflection

As you reflect on your personal study of Song of Songs 7–8, what are the **BEAUTIFUL WORDS** the Holy Spirit has been highlighting to you through this time? Write or draw them in the space below.

SMALL GROUP LEADER'S GUIDE

If you are reading this, you have likely agreed to lead a small group through *Song of Songs*. Thank you! What you have chosen to do is important, and much good fruit can come from studies like this. The rewards of being a leader are different from those of participating, and we hope you find your own walk with Jesus deepened by this experience.

Song of Songs is a seven-session study built around video teaching content and small-group interaction. As the group leader, imagine yourself as the host of a dinner party . . . without dinner, unless of course that's your thing. Your job is to take care of your "guests" so that as they arrive, they feel comfortable and welcomed and excited to learn straightaway.

As the group leader, you are more of a facilitator than a teacher. Your role is NOT to answer all the questions or reteach the content—the video and study guide will do most of that work. Your job is to guide the experience and cultivate your small group into a learning and growing community. This will make it a place for members to process, question, reflect, and grow together.

There are several elements in this leader's guide that will help you as you structure your study and reflection time, so follow along and take advantage of each one.

BEFORE YOU BEGIN

MATERIALS

Before your first meeting, make sure the participants have a copy of this study guide. Alternatively, you can hand out the study guides at your first meeting and give the group members some time to look over the material and ask any preliminary questions. During your first meeting, be sure to send a sheet around the room and have the members write down their names, phone numbers, and email addresses so you can keep in touch with them during the week.

FREE STREAMING VIDEO ACCESS

Additionally, spend a few minutes going over how to access the FREE streaming video using the code printed on the inside front cover of each study guide. Helping everyone understand how accessible this material is will go a long way if anyone (including you) has to miss a meeting or if any member of your group chooses to lead a study after the conclusion of this one!

A few commonly asked questions and answers:

Do I have to subscribe to StudyGateway? NO. If you sign up for StudyGateway for the first time using **studygateway.com/redeem**, you will not be prompted to subscribe, then or after.

Do I set up another account if I do another study later? NO. The next time you do a HarperChristian Resources study with FREE streaming access, all you need to do is enter the new access code and the videos will be added to your account library.

There is a short video available walking through how to access your streaming videos. You can choose to show the video at your first meeting or simply direct your group to the HarperChristian Resources YouTube channel to watch it at their convenience.

HOW TO ACCESS FREE STREAMING VIDEOS: **https://youtu.be/JPhG06ksOn8**

GROUP SIZE

Generally, the ideal size for a group is between eight to ten people, which ensures everyone will have enough time to participate in discussions. If you have more people, you might want to break up the main group into smaller subgroups. Encourage those who show up at the first meeting to commit to attending the duration of the study, as this will help the group members get to know each other, create stability for the group, and help you know how to prepare each week.

OPENING ACTIVITY

Each of the sessions begins with an opening activity to prime the group for deep discussion. Be sure to look ahead at the opening activity for each week so you have the proper materials and, occasionally, can request that each participant bring something to next week's group meeting. Opening activities are meant to get everyone talking, so try to limit each person's comments to one to two minutes so that everyone who wants to can share.

Whenever prompted to select a volunteer to read a passage of any sort, please take the temperature of the room, as it were. Note the members of your group who do not readily raise their hands to volunteer. Reading Scripture aloud can incite anxiety or nervousness in some people. Please take the time in Week 1 to communicate the value of reading Scripture aloud as a community, in community. Encourage all your group members to try it at some point. Be clear that there is no bad reading of God's Word, rather it is meant to be read and shared with others. So, consider your group space a safe place to try and grow in this practice. One goal of this study is to grow participants in their overall engagement of God's Word, which includes feeling comfortable and confident with the words on the pages!

PREPARING YOUR GROUP FOR THE STUDY

Before watching your first video at your first meeting, let the group members know that each session contains three days' worth of Bible study and reflection materials to complete during the week between group meetings. While the personal study is optional, it will help the members cement the concepts presented during the group study time and encourage them to spend time each day in God's Word.

One of the most lamented aspects of all church ministry is struggling to get people to read their Bibles on their own. We have made reading a book of the Bible as simple and engaging as ever, and your group members will not believe what they get out of spending time each week engaging God's Word for themselves!.

Also, invite your group members to bring any questions and insights they uncovered while reading to your next meeting, especially if they had a breakthrough moment or if they didn't understand something.

WEEKLY PREPARATION

As the leader, there are a few things you should do to prepare for each meeting:

- *Watch the video.* This will help you to become familiar with the content Lisa is presenting and give you foresight of what may or may not be brought up in the discussion time.
- *Read through the group discussion section.* This will help you to become familiar with the questions you will be asking, the focus Scripture, and the context. This practice allows you to better anticipate any alterations you might need or want to make in the discussion time for your best group experience.
- *Decide which questions you definitely want to discuss.* Based on the amount and length of group discussion, you may not be able to get through all of the questions, so choose four to five questions that you definitely want to cover.
- *Be familiar with the questions you want to discuss.* Every group has times when there are no respondents and the question falls flat out of the gate. This is normal and okay! Be prepared with YOUR answer to the questions so you can always offer to share as an icebreaker and example. **What you want to avoid is always answering the questions and therefore speaking for the group. Foremost, encourage members of the group to answer questions.**
- *Remind your group there are no wrong answers or dumb questions.* Note that in many cases there will not be one "right" answer to the question. Answers will vary, especially when the group members are being asked to share their personal experiences.

- *Pray for your group.* Pray for your group members throughout the week and ask God to lead them as they study His Word.
- *Bring extra supplies to your meeting.* The members should bring their own pens for writing notes, but it's a good idea to have extras available for those who forget. You may also want to bring paper and additional Bibles.

STRUCTURING THE DISCUSSION TIME

You will need to determine with your group how long you want to meet each week so you can plan your time accordingly. Generally, most groups like to meet for either sixty minutes or ninety minutes, so you could use one of the following schedules:

Section	60 minutes	90 minutes
Introduction (members arrive and get settled; leader reads or summarizes introduction)	2 minutes	2 minutes
Opening Activity	5 minutes	10 minutes
Video Notes (watch the teaching video together and take notes)	35 minutes	35 minutes
Group Discussion (discuss the Bible study questions you selected ahead of time)	15 minutes	40 minutes
Closing Prayer (pray together as a group and dismiss)	3 minutes	3 minutes

As the group leader, it is up to you to keep track of the time and keep things moving along according to your schedule. You might want to set a timer for each segment so both you and the group members know when your time is up. (Note that there are some good phone apps for timers that play a gentle chime or other pleasant sound instead of a disruptive noise.)

Don't be concerned if the group members are quiet or slow to share. People are often quiet when they are pulling together their ideas, and this might be a new experience for them. Just ask a question and let it hang in the air until someone shares. You can then say, "Thank you. What about others? What came to you when you watched that portion of the video?"

GROUP DYNAMICS

Leading a group through *Song of Songs* will prove to be highly rewarding both to you and your group members. However, this doesn't mean you will not encounter any challenges along the way! Discussions can get off track. Group members may not be sensitive to the needs and ideas of others. Some might worry they will be expected to talk about matters that make them feel awkward. Others may express comments that result in disagreements. To help ease this strain on you and the group, consider the following ground rules:

- When someone raises a question or comment that is off the main topic, suggest you deal with it another time, or, if you feel led to go in that direction, let the group know you will be spending some time discussing it.
- If someone asks a question you don't know how to answer, admit it and move on. At your discretion, feel free to invite group members to comment on questions that call for personal experience.
- If you find one or two people are dominating the discussion time, direct a few questions to others in the group. Outside the main group time, ask the more dominating members to help you draw out the quieter ones. Work to make them a part of the solution instead of the problem.
- When a disagreement occurs, encourage the group members to process the matter in love. Encourage those on opposite sides to restate what they heard the other side say about the matter, and then invite each side to evaluate if that perception is accurate. Lead the group in examining other Scriptures related to the topic and look for common ground.

When any of these issues arise, encourage your group members to follow these words from the Bible: "Love one another" (John 13:34), "If it is possible, as far as it depends on you, live at peace with everyone" (Romans 12:18), and "Be quick to listen, slow to speak and slow to become angry" (James 1:19). This will make your group time more rewarding and beneficial for everyone who attends.

SESSION ONE: INTO ME YOU SEE

Description: This first session provides participants with an overview of Song of Songs, discussing interpretive methods, major themes, and preparing the group for personal study.

Scripture covered in this session: **Jeremiah 2:1–2; Isaiah 54:5–7; Ephesians 5:25, 32; Revelation 19:6–8; Luke 24:13, 21, 27; Song of Songs 1:2–4**
Scripture during personal study days: **Song of Songs 1:1–4**

Verse of the Week: "Let him kiss me with the kisses of his mouth—for your love is more delightful than wine" (Song of Songs 1:2).

Discussion Question choices / notes: ______________________

____

PRAYER REQUESTS

SESSION TWO: STOPPED IN YOUR TRACKS

Description: This session invites participants to consider Shulamite's perspective in Song of Songs chapter 1, exploring her insecurity in her relationship and Solomon's public declarations of their love.

Scripture covered in this session: **Song of Songs 1:5–6, 8–10, 15; 2:3**
Scripture during personal study days: **Song of Songs 1**

Verse of the Week: "Let him lead me to the banquet hall, and let his banner over me be love" (Song of Songs 2:4).

Discussion Question choices / notes: ______________________

____

PRAYER REQUESTS

SESSION THREE: SUITORS WHO RUN AND FOXES WHO RUIN

Description: This session asks participants to contemplate the image of Solomon leaping toward his beloved and picture God running toward us. It also challenges us to identify the "little foxes" that can interrupt our relationship with Jesus.

Scripture covered in this session: **Song of Songs 2:8–12, 15–17; Luke 15:11–20; Proverbs 4:23**
Scripture during personal study days: **Song of Songs 2**

Verse of the Week: "Look! Here he comes, leaping across the mountains, bounding over the hills" (Song of Songs 2:8).

Discussion Question choices / notes: ______

PRAYER REQUESTS

SESSION FOUR: A BREATHLESS SEARCH AND A BIG PARADE

Description: This session invites participants to experience Shulamite's desperate search for Solomon and subsequent wedding parade and ceremony. It connects Solomon's ascent to Shulamite with the pillar of God's presence in Exodus.

Scripture covered in this session: **Song of Songs 3:1–4, 6–11; Exodus 13:21–22; the Psalms of Ascent**
Scripture during personal study days: **Song of Songs 3**

Verse of the Week: "Look on King Solomon wearing a crown, the crown with which his mother crowned him on the day of his wedding, the day his heart rejoiced" (Song of Songs 3:11b).

Discussion Question choices / notes: ______

PRAYER REQUESTS

SESSION FIVE: THE PINNACLE OF PASSION

Description: This session explores the power of passion and affection and shows the parallels to Jesus as our Divine Bridegroom.

Scripture covered in this session: **Song of Songs 4:1–5, 9, 16**
Scripture during personal study days: **Song of Songs 4**

Verse of the Week: "You have stolen my heart, my sister, my bride; you have stolen my heart with one glance of your eyes, with one jewel of your necklace" (Song of Songs 4:9).

Discussion Question choices / notes: ______________________________

____

PRAYER REQUESTS

SESSION SIX: WHEN DELIGHT TURNS TO DRUDGERY

Description: This session explores the moment in Shulamite and Solomon's relationship that betrays a sense of daily drudgery and Shulamite's recounting of Solomon's goodness. It parallels our relationship with God, inviting us to recount our blessings and His goodness in our lives.

Scripture covered in this session: **Song of Songs 5:2–8, 10–16; Joshua 3:7–13; 4:21–24**
Scripture during personal study days: **Song of Songs 5–6**

Verse of the Week: "Daughters of Jerusalem, I charge you—if you find my beloved, what will you tell him? Tell him I am faint with love" (Song of Songs 5:8).

Discussion Question choices / notes: ______________________________

____

PRAYER REQUESTS

SESSION SEVEN: SEALED WITH SECURITY

Description: This final session invites participants to contemplate the ways security in a relationship can bring confidence and contentment. The session points us to the culmination of Song of Songs in the declaration of unconditional love between Solomon and Shulamite, paralleling God's unconditional love for us.

Scripture covered in this session: **Song of Songs 7:7–9; 8:5–10; Luke 8:1–3; Ephesians 3:14–19**
Scripture during personal study days: **Song of Songs 7–8**

Verse of the Week: "Many waters cannot quench love; rivers cannot sweep it away. If one were to give all the wealth of one's house for love, it would be utterly scorned" (Song of Songs 8:7).

Discussion Question choices / notes:

PRAYER REQUESTS

SCRIPTURE MEMORY CARDS

SESSION 1

Let him kiss me with the kisses of his mouth—for your love is more delightful than wine.

Song of Songs 1:2

SESSION 2

Let him lead me to the banquet hall, and let his banner over me be love.

Song of Songs 2:4

SESSION 3

Look! Here he comes, leaping across the mountains, bounding over the hills.

Song of Songs 2:8

SESSION 4

Look on King Solomon wearing a crown, the crown with which his mother crowned him on the day of his wedding, the day his heart rejoiced.

Song of Songs 3:11b

SCRIPTURE MEMORY CARDS

SESSION 5

You have stolen my heart, my sister, my bride; you have stolen my heart with one glance of your eyes, with one jewel of your necklace.

Song of Songs 4:9

SESSION 6

Daughters of Jerusalem, I charge you—if you find my beloved, what will you tell him? Tell him I am faint with love.

Song of Songs 5:8

SESSION 7

Many waters cannot quench love; rivers cannot sweep it away. If one were to give all the wealth of one's house for love, it would be utterly scorned.

Song of Songs 8:7

ENDNOTES

1. Jonathan Kaplan. "The Holy of Holies or the Holiest? Rabbi Akiva's Characterization of Song of Songs in Mishnah Yadayim 3:5," in *"It's Better to Hear the Rebuke of the Wise than the Song of Fools" (Qoh 7:5): Proceedings of the Midrash Section, Society of Biblical Literature* 6, (2016): https://www.degruyterbrill.com/document/doi/10.31826/9781463236809-004/html.
2. Kaplan. "The Holy of Holies."
3. Madame Guyon. *A Short and Easy Method of Prayer: Discovering Peace and Intimacy through Fellowship with God* (1685).
4. A. W. Tozer. *The Knowledge of the Holy: The Attributes of God: Their Meaning in the Christian Life* (HarperOne, 1978), 1.
5. *Bible Hub.* "1 Kings 4:1." https://biblehub.com/study/1_kings/4-1.htm#:~:text=19%2D21).-,ruled%20over%20Israel,3:9%2D12).
6. Origen. *The Song of Songs, Commentary and Homilies: Ancient Christian Writers* (The Newman Press, 1957).
7. *Merriam-Webster Dictionary.* "Verdant." https://www.merriam-webster.com/dictionary/verdant.
8. Watchman Nee. *The Song of Songs: The Divine Romance Between God & Man* (Living Stream Ministry, 1995).
9. Nadine Epstein. *Elie Wiesel, An Extraordinary Life and Legacy: Writings, Photographs and Reflections* (MomentBooks, 2019).
10. Watchman Nee. *Song of Songs: Unveiling the Mystery of Passionate Intimacy with Christ* (CLC Publications, 2006).
11. Nee. *Song of Songs: Unveiling the Mystery.*
12. *Bible Gateway.* "Theophany." https://www.biblegateway.com/resources/encyclopedia-of-the-bible/Theophany.
13. Helen Howarth Lemmel, "Turn Your Eyes Upon Jesus," 1922.
14. M. G. Easton. *Easton's Bible Dictionary* (CreateSpace Independent Publishing Platform, 2015).
15. R. S. Hess. *Song of Songs* (Baker Academic, 2017).
16. Dr. Robertson McQuilkin. *A Promise Kept* (Tyndale House Publishers, 1998).

ABOUT THE AUTHOR

Rarely are the terms "hilarious storyteller" and "theologian" used in the same sentence—much less to describe the same person—but Lisa Harper is definitely not stereotypical! She has an earned doctorate from Houston Theological Seminary, has published extensively, and teaches the Bible around the world, but she's also a frequent belly laugher. She describes her greatest accomplishment as being Missy's mom through the miracle of adoption, followed closely by learning to wake surf in her sixties.

Also Available From Lisa

Risking Everything Is So Worth It

In this eight-session study, Lisa reveals how the Holy Spirit catapults believers forward with power, grace, and authority to dramatically impact the world.

Move Beyond Facts and Experience the Fullness of God

In this seven-session study, Lisa invites you to explore the depths of God's character, His love for us, and how biblically sound theology deepens our relationships with God and each other.

Advent Is Not the End

In this four-session study taught with Christine Caine you will recapture the wonder of Jesus' obvious love for you and discover that Advent is a reason to share the hope of Jesus throughout the year.

Easter Is So Much More than a Holiday

In this four-session study taught with Christine Caine your understanding of Easter will be transformed beyond tradition toward daily living that celebrates and activates the power of Christ's Resurrection.